AF647633

RED ROAD ACROSS THE GREAT PLAINS

CHANDRA LAHIRI

Dawn Voyager

Copyright © 2019 Chandra Lahiri

The right of Chandra Lahiri to be identified as the author
of this Work has been asserted by him in accordance
with the Copyright, Designs and Patents Act 1988.

First published in 2019
by Dawn Voyager www.dawnvoyager.com

ISBN: 978-93-5391-234-5

Apart from any use permitted under USA or UK copyright law, this publication may only be reproduced, stored or transmitted, in any form, or by any means, with the prior permission, of the author.

Every effort has been made to fulfil requirements for reproducing copyright material. The Author is glad to rectify any inadvertent omissions.

Front cover: Crazy Horse Memorial, Black Hills
Back cover: Native Memorial, Little Bighorn Battlefield

Printed at global locations by Lightning Source, and distributed worldwide (paperback & e-book) by Ingram Content Group, One Ingram Boulevard, La Vergne, TN 37086, U.S.A

BISAC: TRV001000, HIS028000, EDU016000, SOC021000

NON-FICTION: TRAVEL, HISTORY, NATIVE AMERICAN

DEDICATION

This book is dedicated to all the "Invisible Warriors", on and off the Native American Reservations, who are fighting such a heroic battle, against unbelievable odds, to reclaim their heritage and build a brighter future.

Get involved! Take a stand! Start by visiting:
www.cloudhorseartinstitute.org
&
www.ocetiwakan.org

If you enjoy this book, you can view over 700 color photographs, more than 60 videos, maps, and much other material from this odyssey, by visiting www.dawnvoyager.com.

CONTENTS

ACKNOWLEDGEMENTS

"Then he was told:
Remember what you have seen,
Because everything forgotten
Returns to the circling winds"
~~ Navajo Wind Chant

An army of people made this, the last, and greatest adventure of my life possible. It is often difficult to get Native Americans to talk freely, due not only to the very real, generational cultural and spiritual trauma that still haunts many, especially on the less-assimilated northern Plains but also because that heritage has sometimes become clouded and hazy through the indoctrination of the victors. With a natural reserve and exceptional gravitas, they prefer to listen rather than speak. Interrupting someone speaking, or rushing to respond without adequate time for reflection, is deeply offensive. I first noticed this at the Canyon de Chelley, on the Navajo Reservation. Our Navajo guide was friendly and very well informed, but chatty he was not. And yet, one of my major objectives was to get to know them, to gain some insight into their lives today and their perspective of the past.

Providentially, the vital break in the logjam came from our friend, Carol Rizzardi, a one-time fellow teacher of my wife's. One of the most open-minded, intellectual and enthusiastic social consciences I have had the privilege of knowing, she was an early supporter—who just had a Dakota friend with links to the Pine Ridge Reservation! Rondell Clay, who now works for a Native American

NGO in Washington D.C. put me in touch with Cindy Catches, wife of the respected Lakota Medicine Man, Peter V. Catches. I was privileged to meet this remarkable couple just a few days before Peter passed on to join the grandfathers in the beyond.

The Internet introduced me to another extraordinary couple, Mark and Tilda St. Pierre of Red Owl Springs, near Kyle on the Pine Ridge Reservation. Along with others like Stella Iron Cloud, they showed me that self-help, positivity in adversity, and undaunted hope for the future are alive and well on the Reservation, contrary to popular urban legends. The Internet also introduced me to Vernell White Thunder, owner of the White Thunder Ranch on the Reservation, who showed me around sacred Bear Butte and brought me one of the most subtly mystical experiences of my life. A truly fine gentleman if ever I met one.

The Internet located several Native American publications and the then-Editor of the "Native American Times" (now Editor of "Native Oklahoma"), Lisa Hicks Snell, generously guided this acolyte in the ways of contemporary Native life. Among publications, I received encouragement from Cat Whipple, Managing Editor of "The Circle", though I never got to meet her. In the best journalistic tradition, the world over, all the other publications simply ignored me. Most Native government bodies I contacted by email also offered the traditional silence of bureaucrats around the globe.

Carney Saupitty Jr., Cultural Specialist at the Comanche National Museum at Lawton, Oklahoma talked extensively about contemporary life and times of the Comanche—despite undoubtedly having answered the same questions for hundreds of visitors every day. His generosity of spirit was inspirational, and I have tried to emulate his attitude, however much a challenge it was at times. His optimism, willingness to forgive past sins and move towards a future of reconciliation and reconstruction were symptomatic of the new uplifted spirit infusing the Great Plains.

The biggest tip of the hat goes to my beloved wife, Rajyashri (Keya) Lahiri, the only family member who read all 22 of the original articles published in the "Muscat Daily" newspaper of Oman, where we live. Despite grave reservations about a "broken-down old man" traversing alone the wild, remote badlands of mid-America, depicted in so many terrifying Hollywood movies, she put on a brave face and supported me all the way - though, I suspect, she finally succumbed to the delightful prospect of having me out of her hair for an entire month. My two Sons, Mayank and Shaon, and Shaon's wife, Nupur, always encouraged me and kept the faith. Without my wonderful family, this quest would have been barely a wistful figment of my imagination.

Any errors of understanding or interpreting Native American heritage or culture are entirely mine, and for them, I would, with humility, seek the forbearance of the People. I have tried my utmost, with honesty and sincerity, to tread the Red Road with an open heart and a keen desire to learn. If I have succeeded even a little, it will have been one of the most worthwhile endeavors of my life. If I have failed, it was not for lack of passion or effort!

FOREWORD

*"Our destination is never a place, but rather
a new way of looking at things."*
~~ Henry Miller

"Yes, I know they lost their land. So what? Aren't they getting money from the Government? It's time they stopped whining and got on with their lives!"

The impatient comment of my good friend was so wrong, on so many levels, it sent an immediate, blinding flash of anger coursing through me. Then, I recollected my elder Son's similar, much kinder and very reasonable query, "Pa, why are they in such bad shape on the Reservations? They live in the land of opportunity, don't need visas or green cards to work in the world's greatest economy. Why don't they just go out across the country and build great lives?"

It was a perfectly valid question and got me thinking. Even my friend's outburst, I realized, stemmed from the deplorable lack of accurate information out in the world about the Native American experience – even in America.

Why I wondered, am I so passionate about them, anyway? I am from half a world away, with no tangible link to them. And yet, my feelings have always run far deeper than mere curiosity. It has disturbed me for almost a half-century, and I hoped this pilgrimage would help me find some answers. In the event, it did not. The thirst is unquenched.

It was an Indian summer three times over – besides being a rendezvous with Native Indians, I am an Indian too ("a dot Indian, not a feather Indian," as one innocently put it), and the weather on the southern Great Plains was hot enough to be an Indian summer.

As for the Red Road, in Native American spirituality, the Black Road is for conflict, difficulties, treachery, dissonance; the Red Road is for peace, love, enlightenment, happiness, positivity, traveled by an open mind. I believe I drove the Red.

Like children everywhere, I remember many excited games of Cowboys & Indians. The cowboys were always the good guys, the Indians the bad ones, and there was robust competition to be a cowboy. Strangely, even then, I recall preferring to be an Indian. It was a jolt, in later life, to discover that, in reality, the good and bad guys were frequently the opposite. Cowboys had limited contact with Indians most of the time. So much for John Wayne! One more childhood icon bites the dust.

I became deeply, then passionately, engrossed in Native American history and heritage in my later school years, and it has not left me over the past half-century. My interest has deepened and my feelings are mysteriously more emotional. One of the few paper books I have kept, of my now-defunct large bookworm's library, in this Kindle age, is a very tattered, annotated, lovingly Scotch-taped copy of Dee Brown's seminal "Bury My Heart at Wounded Knee", received as a prize for something or other at School. It was pivotal in my life. Since then, I have read, researched, watched, been frustrated by, and animatedly debated, the subject of Native Americans to the edge of insanity!

It was many years later, at 63, after I had retired, that I finally had the leisure to consider visiting the Great Plains and perhaps meeting some of the people I had grown to care about so much. My vague ideas gradually took shape, and a plan began to emerge from the mists. Yes, why not!

I am not sure when it became really serious but gradually, I worked up a once-in-a-lifetime, month-long, solo pilgrimage across the Great Plains, visiting many of the decisive sites of their story, spending time on the Reservations and, above all, getting to know some of them. What started as an idle retiree's fantasy rapidly took on a life of its own, almost as though by some divine will.

Over the next year, I dug in, researching, reading, watching videos, planning, and scheming. It grew into a 6000-kilometer run from Tulsa, Oklahoma, through Kansas, Nebraska, South Dakota, Montana and Wyoming to the Yellowstone National Park. For an old (oldish, I prefer) man venturing into unknown territories all on his own, it was not only slightly audacious but perhaps even downright foolhardy, as alarmed friends and family repeatedly admonished me. Had I learned nothing from all the Hollywood movies that showed just how dangerous the red-neck, rural heartland of America is? Deaf to the well-intentioned advice, I decided to risk whatever the throw of the dice might bring. Something was pushing me inexorably onto the red road.

The odyssey would take me to the Cherokee, Comanche, Southern Cheyenne, Northern Cheyenne, and Lakota, besides the storied Wild West towns of Dodge City and Deadwood. I would grieve over blood-soaked massacre sites, celebrate on battlefields of triumph, and contemplate the deservedly sacred Black Hills. Finally, I would rendezvous with my wife in Buffalo Bill's town of Cody and spend the last few days exploring the Yellowstone National Park.

While I sprinkled in a few oddities, such as a detour to the Minuteman Missile silos, the site of the massive collection of Mammoth skeletons in the Black Hills, and that heaven of kitsch, the Wall Drug Store, it was, primarily, a very focused exploration of Native American heritage and the Old Frontier. Eventually, I covered almost 5800 kms (approximately 3600 miles), in 100 hours of driving, burnt 427 liters of 'gas' (petrol to us ignorant non-Americans), wore out 4 tires and 3 pens, earned 1 substantial speeding fine, crossed 6 States and 3 time zones. Doing it solo was not so much for adventure as it was because of sheer necessity. As my wife put it, finding similarly insane companions is challenging!

I have avoided the moniker "Indians", bestowed on them by a confused, lost European, and other, often pejorative, European labels like "Sioux". These are inaccurate and frequently as offensive as the appropriation of their culture by American football teams. They are Lakota, Cheyenne, Cherokee, Apache... I am mystified why some of them still accept being addressed otherwise, even amongst themselves.

Deeply disheartening, the ill-treatment of and discrimination against Native Americans is rampant even today. While a kindlier Canada has rarely massacred or hounded its Native population with brute force, it is not alien to that mindset either. This discrimination stems from ignorance and apathy, probably with a dash of inherited guilt.

It is important to state upfront that, though I am unabashedly for the underdog, this is not a sob story, an unqualified paean to the Native American, or a rant against white America. I have always been a great admirer of America, a nation that, despite its blemishes, never needed to be made great again. The America I admire is the America of the Marshall Plan; the America whose welcome to the world was, "Give me your tired, your poor, your huddled masses yearning to breathe free"; the America of "We, the People"; the America that nursed the crippled Apollo 13 safely home; the America of Martin Luther King Jr.; the America that, I firmly believe, will finally accept its Native American inheritance and stretch forth its bounteous hand to bring them, too, into the American Dream. Near the end of his life, Crazy Horse prophesied that the seventh generation after his would bring healing to the Nations. We are now amidst the seventh generation, and the first tender green shoots of this healing are already evident.

I am awed by the United States achieving economic, political, and military pre-eminence in the world within just two centuries – something never achieved in human history. To me, the American Dream is opportunity, innovation and, above all, hope. The inescapable, tragic irony is that no Native ever objected to the white man sharing his land, or taking the gold, oil, and coal, for which he had no use. All he desired was for his buffalo to be left alone, and for him to live as he always had. It is well past time the American mainstream acknowledged history and enabled their

Native peoples to participate, unfettered, in the American Century. The tired stereotype of the substance-abusing, alcoholic, suicidal Native living in abject misery, is making way for the new stories of starter wins and little triumphs. I recognize the dark centuries of genocide, but also see the glorious sunrise tingeing the dawn. The seventh generation is at work!

In cultural or spiritual matters, the more I am exposed to them, the more I am humbled by how little I know or understand. I embarked with more appreciation than an understanding of the Native vision. It is overwhelming to realize just how rich and intricate their spirituality really is, woven seamlessly into the texture of their everyday existence, especially contrasted with the abject poverty of my own soul, shackled inexorably by the chains of Western scientific conditioning. In the end, this is simply a record of one man's pilgrimage – sometimes funny, occasionally tragic, frequently eye-opening, and ultimately, hopeful of the future of these remarkable people – my own "Canterbury Tales."

Chandra Lahiri

Muscat, Sultanate of Oman

September-December, 2018

TIMELINE: PEOPLE

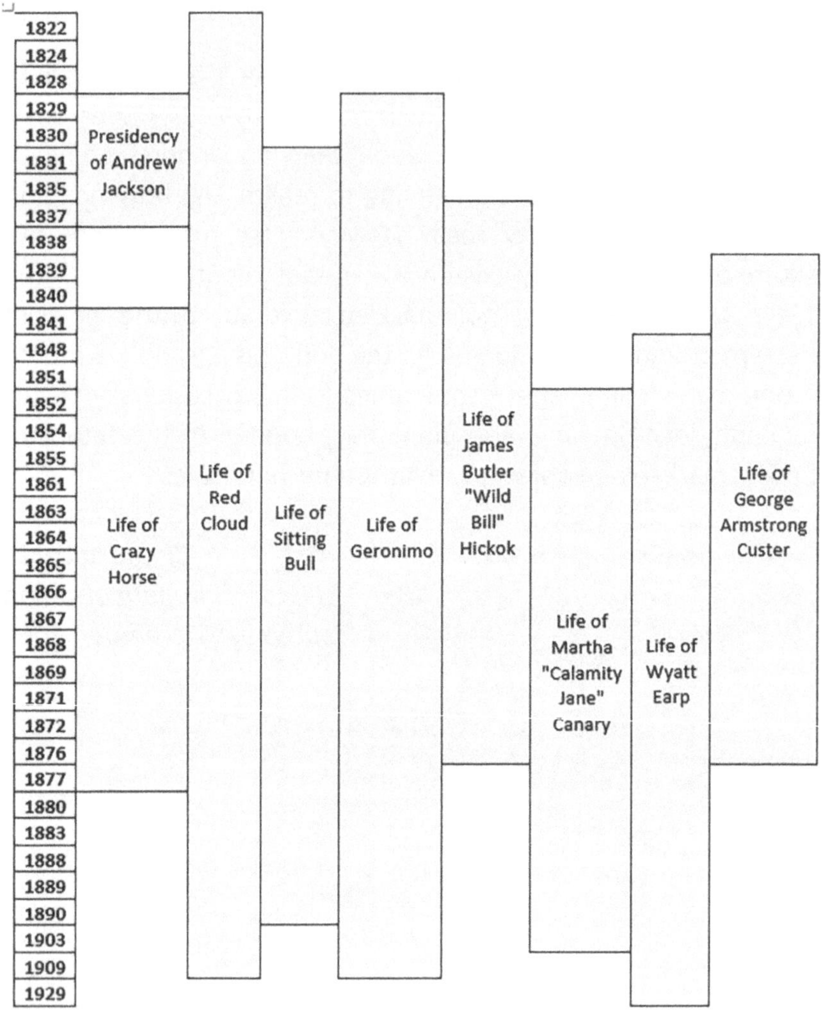

TIMELINE: EVENTS

<table>
<tr><td>1819</td><td>Civilization Fund Act</td><td></td><td></td><td></td><td></td><td></td></tr>
<tr><td>1821</td><td></td><td></td><td></td><td></td><td rowspan="18">Santa Fe Trail</td><td></td></tr>
<tr><td>1824</td><td></td><td></td><td rowspan="18">Fort Gibson</td><td></td><td></td></tr>
<tr><td>1830</td><td>Indian Removal Act</td><td></td><td></td><td></td></tr>
<tr><td>1835</td><td>New Echota Treaty</td><td></td><td></td><td></td></tr>
<tr><td>1838</td><td>Trail of Tears</td><td></td><td></td><td></td></tr>
<tr><td>1851</td><td>Horse Creek Treaty</td><td></td><td></td><td></td></tr>
<tr><td>1854</td><td>Grattan Fight</td><td></td><td></td><td></td></tr>
<tr><td>1855</td><td>Blue Water Massacre</td><td></td><td></td><td></td></tr>
<tr><td>1863</td><td></td><td rowspan="3">American Civil War</td><td rowspan="6">Bozeman Trail</td><td></td></tr>
<tr><td>1864</td><td>Sand Creek Massacre</td><td></td></tr>
<tr><td>1865</td><td></td><td></td></tr>
<tr><td>1866</td><td>Fetterman Battle</td><td></td><td></td></tr>
<tr><td>1867</td><td>Wagonbox Fight</td><td rowspan="5">Chisholm Trail</td><td></td></tr>
<tr><td>1868</td><td>Washita Massacre</td><td>Treaty of Laramie</td></tr>
<tr><td>1869</td><td></td><td rowspan="12">Fort Sill</td><td></td></tr>
<tr><td>1871</td><td>Red Cloud Agency established</td><td></td></tr>
<tr><td>1872</td><td>Founding of Dodge City</td><td></td></tr>
<tr><td>1876</td><td>Battles of Rosebud & Little Bighorn</td><td>Founding of Deadwood</td><td></td></tr>
<tr><td>1883</td><td></td><td>Native religions banned - Code of Indian Offences</td><td></td><td></td></tr>
<tr><td>1889</td><td></td><td>General Allotment Act</td><td></td><td></td><td></td></tr>
<tr><td>1890</td><td>Wounded Knee Massacre</td><td>Dawes Roll</td><td></td><td></td><td></td></tr>
<tr><td>1930</td><td></td><td rowspan="2">Kansas Dustbowl</td><td></td><td></td><td></td></tr>
<tr><td>1936</td><td></td><td></td><td></td><td></td></tr>
<tr><td>1973</td><td>Wounded Knee (AIM)</td><td></td><td></td><td></td><td></td></tr>
<tr><td>1978</td><td>Indian Child Welfare Act</td><td>American Indian Religious Freedom Act</td><td></td><td></td><td></td></tr>
<tr><td>Present</td><td></td><td></td><td></td><td></td><td></td></tr>
</table>

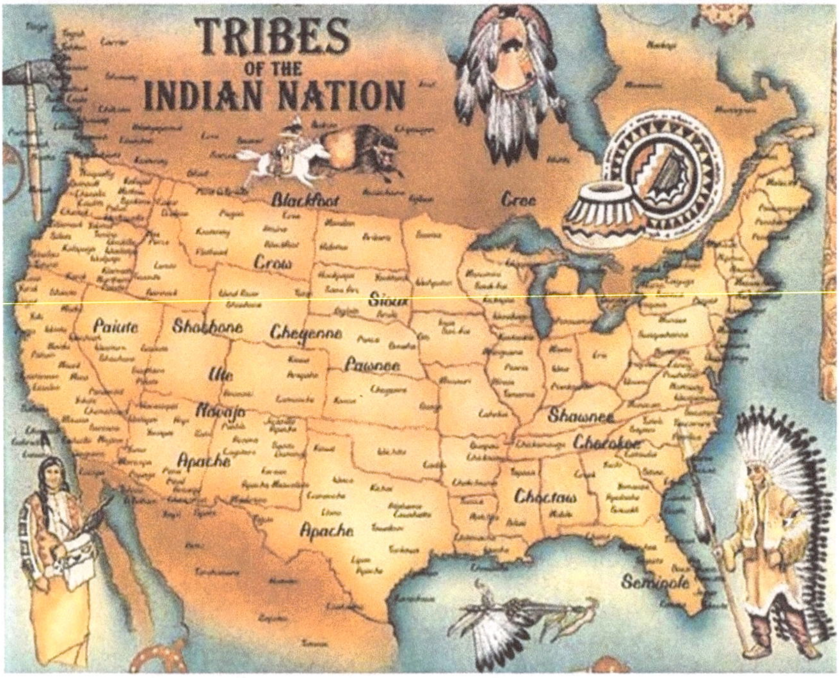

Courtesy: https://oldwestdailyreader.com/native-american-tribes/

Indian Reservations 1890
CANADA
WASHINGTON
OREGON
IDAHO
MONTANA
WYOMING
N. DAK
S. DAK.
MINN
WIS.
MICH.
IOWA
ILL.
NEBRASKA
NEVADA
UTAH TERR.
COLORADO
KANSAS
MISSOURI
KY.
TENN.
ARK.
MISS.
LA.
TEXAS
CALIFORNIA
ARIZONA TERR.
NEW MEXICO TERR.
OKLA. TERR.
INDIAN TERR.
ROCKY MOUNTAINS
GREAT PLAINS
PACIFIC OCEAN
MEXICO
Blackfoot
Bear Paw Mtn.
Sioux
Nez Perce
Whitebird Creek
Crow
Little Bighorn
Rosebud
Modoc
Modoc War
Northern Shoshoni
Cheyenne
Black Hills
Wounded Knee
Northern Paiute
Western Shoshoni
Eastern Shoshoni
Ft. Laramie 1854, 1868
Arapaho
Beecher Island
Ute
Southern Paiute
Medicine Lodge 1867
Navajo
Hopi
Jicarilla Apache
Adobe Walls
Zuñi
Cherokee
Creek
Seminole
Chickasaw
Choctaw
Comanche
Washita
Chiricahua Apache
Apache Pass
Mescalero Apache
Major battle
Treaty site
Reservation in 1890
0 150 300 mi
0 150 300 km
© eMapshop

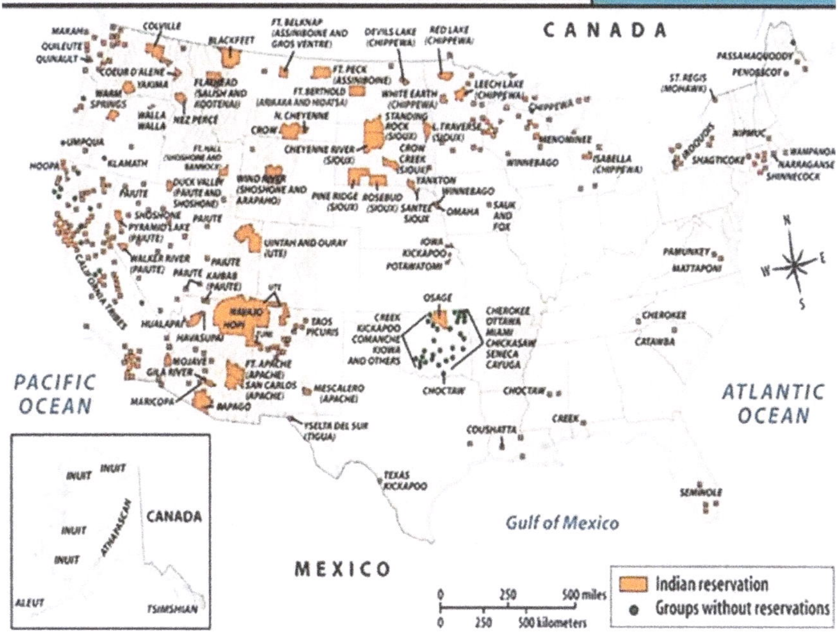
CANADA
PACIFIC OCEAN
ATLANTIC OCEAN
Gulf of Mexico
MEXICO
Indian reservation
Groups without reservations
0 250 500 miles
0 250 500 kilometers

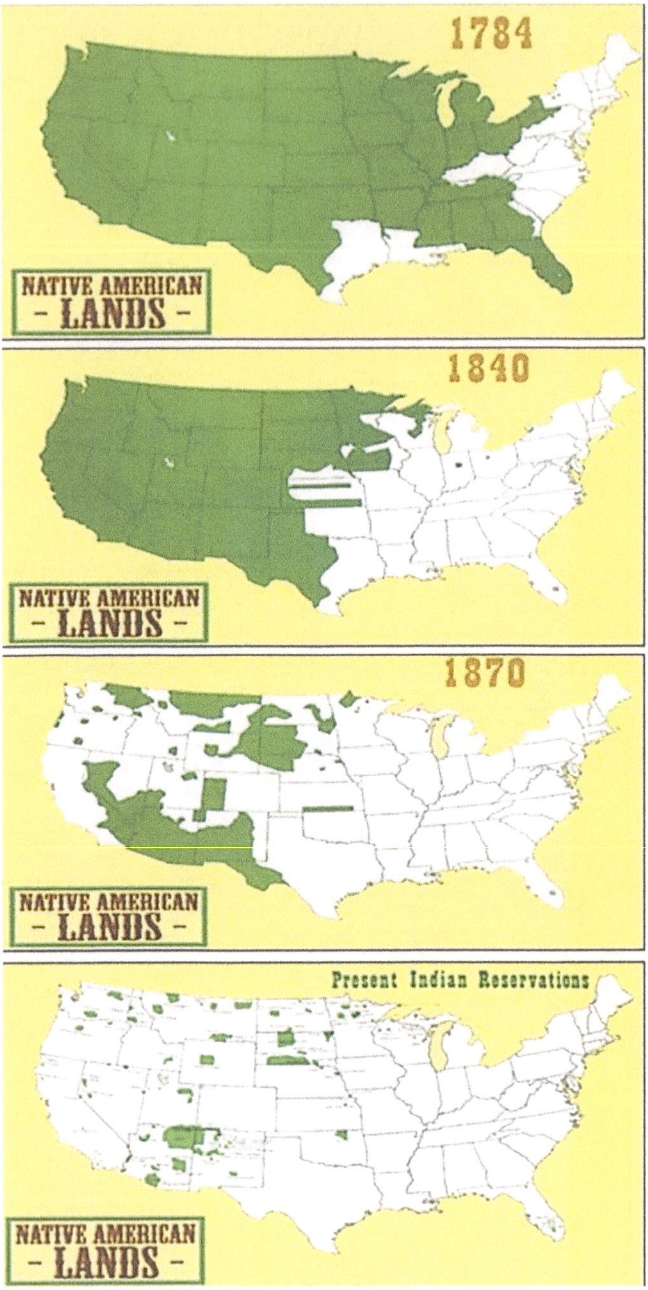

THE VANISHING LANDS

Courtesy: Prof. Sam B Hilliard, Louisiana State University

DAY 0: 20 MAY - DAWN

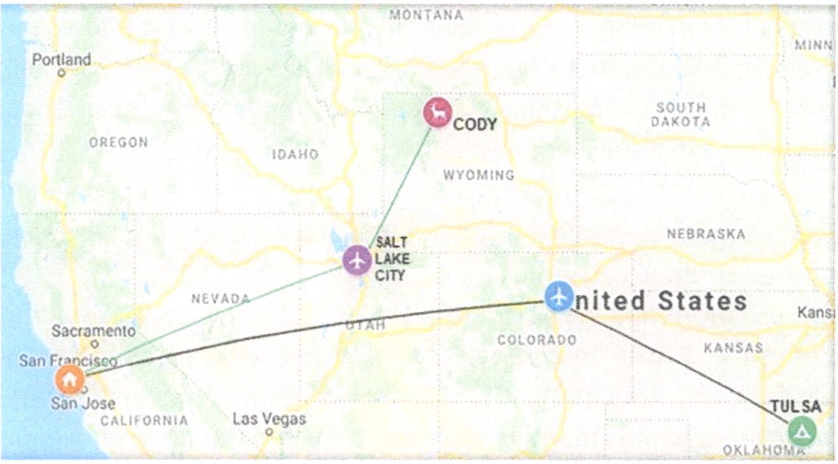

Tomorrow will be the day! After the long months of preparation and decades of reading, I am finally about to hit the open road, on my epic Native American odyssey, right across the legend-saturated, elegiac Great Plains. I am filled with excited anticipation – and, perhaps, just a little trepidation. I will venture into territories I have never visited and know little about, other than from myth and legend. And, if truth be told, I am also slightly apprehensive of rejection, as a stranger, by the people I have loved so long from afar.

Tomorrow, I shall collect my little Ford Focus from Avis, in Tulsa, Oklahoma, and head down the Broken Arrow Expressway, into the heart of "Indian Territory", on my voyage of discovery. Driving this long road-trip all alone will also be something of a voyage of self-discovery, I suspect.

Somewhere I read, "North America is the land of great and mysterious civilizations, whose roots grow deep into the soil." Indeed, I do not know of any culture, besides the Native Americans, whose ties to the soil, and to Nature, are as deep, pervasive and uniquely intertwined into their daily lives. Mother Earth, Father Sky and the Four Directions have immense significance and impact on all our lives. Their spirituality comprehends this. They believe humans are just transient travelers through this world and must respect everything in it. All things in this world serve a purpose in our lives and are, therefore, sacred. This is one of the reasons inter-tribal conflicts were almost always over food and grazing lands; never for territorial conquests.

I am bursting to explore this unusual culture, with the opportunity to do so all the way from the 'diluted' contemporary inheritance of the southern Plains Nations, such as the Cherokee, to the 'purer', more nativist northern Plains Nations, like the Lakota and Cheyenne, whose fierce Dog Soldier warrior society was feared by all. Curiously, though the Comanche, the ultimate horse-meisters, killed more whites than anyone else, it was the Northern Cheyenne (Saheliyas) who suffered more than anyone else.

The old Frontier towns of the Wild West, Dodge City, and Deadwood, I expect, will give me a glimpse of the immense clash of cultures that shaped not just the mid-1800s but the future of America. Were the Natives really the bloody savages, attacking bucolic settlers without warning, as expounded by the propagators of Manifest Destiny, who ensured that the baldly stated aim of the Government of the day would be to either eradicate everything "Indian" in the Natives or erase them from the face of the earth? Or were they simply fighting for the lives of their people and the survival of their civilization? Those who echoed General Sheridan's infamous words, "The only good Indian I ever saw was a dead Indian", or those who agreed with General Crook's supremely honest response to a newspaper reporter's question on the hardest thing about fighting them, "Knowing you are wrong"?

With tribes like the Cherokee, the white man largely succeeded in remaking them in his own image. With others, like the Lakota, less so. Ultimately, white men's diseases destroyed more Natives than did bullets or indoctrination, well beyond the settlers' initial reach, and the job was finished off by the Northern Pacific Railroad, the "final solution" Sherman had predicted, which brought an avalanche of buffalo hunters to the Great Plains, wiping out all the massive herds that used to blanket the land, from horizon to far horizon, the most numerous large animal to ever exist on earth. This was part of the scorched earth or Total War, policy the US Army and Government considered legitimate, after they failed to win the shooting war. The military stalemate was unsurprising since the Natives, especially the Lakota, Comanche, and Cheyenne, were widely respected as the finest cavalry in the world, saluted even by Army soldiers who had faced them in battle, and survived, such as General Anson Mills, on the Rosebud.

Many of the early fur traders, the Mountain Men, especially the French-Canadians who would become the mixed-blood meiti, developed a great respect for the Tribes they came into contact with, and often 'went native' by wholeheartedly embracing their lifestyle and religion, frequently taking Native wives and living in their villages. Turncoats, like the half-breed interpreter Frank Grouard, and Kit Carson, were the exceptions rather than the rule. Other than a few tribes, like the Blackfeet, Native Americans welcomed and readily accepted outsiders into the family.

However, when such respect and understanding extended to enlightened US Army officers, it usually meant an end to their career. General George Crook, though he never forgave Crazy Horse for his defeat on the Rosebud, was the senior-most such officer, and his growing sensitivity to the plight of the Natives ensured his career withered on the vine. The shining heroes of the Civil War, such as General Sherman (Atlanta), General Sheridan (Shenandoah) and Lieutenant Colonel George Armstrong Custer, would all disgrace themselves in the Indian Wars, staining the reputation of the US Army by their attitudes, battle actions, and blatantly untruthful reporting. As Bray succinctly expressed it, "Sheridan was adept at cruising the zeitgeist." Indeed, the notorious Manifest Destiny was enthusiastically propounded by no less a luminary than Colonel Stephen Kearney, celebrated Father of the Dragoons, in whose honor forts would be named around the country. The senior officers who abused the Natives the most hid under the age-old defense of the military criminal, of "following orders." Even the best of them, Crook, who wished to be seen as a man of action and few words, once claimed that his soldiers only fought the tribes when fired upon! The ghosts of Sand Creek, Washita and the many other massacres by the US Army must have stirred at those words. However, even the much-reviled General Nelson "Bear Coat" Miles, reluctantly admitted, "The Indian problem can only be solved by the fulfillment by Congress of the treaty obligations the Indians were entreated and coerced into signing. They signed away their land...for which they received nothing."

In an exquisite irony, General William Tecumseh Sherman, named after the great Shawnee Chief who tried to rally the Seminoles and others against the invaders, was the person who ultimately suppressed those very Nations.

Most treaties stated piously, 'The Government of the United States desires peace, and its honor is hereby pledged to keep it. The Indians desire peace and they now pledge their honor to maintain it." All affirmed, "In God we trust." As events proved, only one side apparently had either honor or trust in their God.

The most important of the Treaties claimed the US Government would honor them "as long as the grass grows, and the rivers flow." I look forward to discovering if the grasses are still growing, and the rivers still flowing, across the Great Plains...

As the famous Lakota war-cry goes, "Hoka-hey!"

DAY 1: 21 MAY - WESTWARD HO!

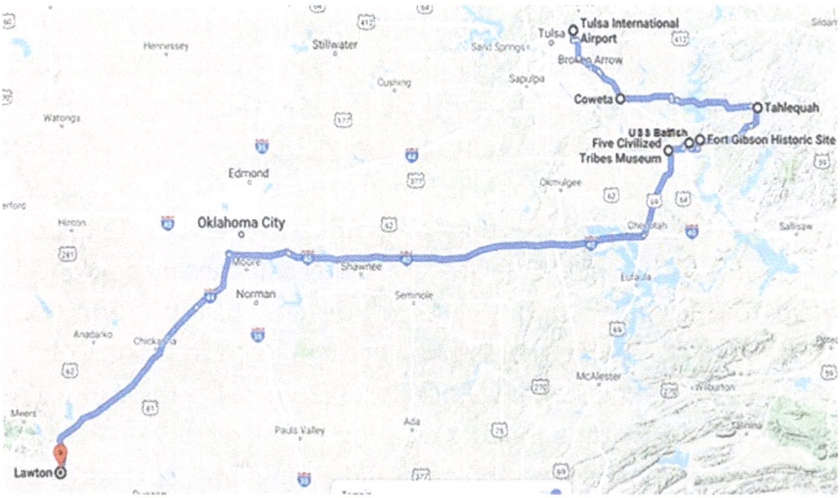

The blinding glint off the aircraft's wing, much like the menacing flash of a Colt Peacemaker wakes me. I am actually traveling Eastward Ho! It has been a long haul across three time zones, via the Mile-High city of Denver (built, incidentally, on land guaranteed by the 1851 Fort Laramie Treaty to the Arapaho, valid even today), to the heart of the storied "Indian Territory", the stuff of sagas and ballads. As the Southwest Airlines jet makes its final approach to Tulsa International Airport in Oklahoma, I am on pins and needles to begin my long-cherished Native American odyssey, following an infrequently trodden route, across six States, from Tulsa to the Yellowstone National Park, vertically across the heartland of America, through the dramatic missteps of history that are these Great Plains. Though history is written by the victors, it cannot be authentic if it is exclusively so. My objective is to absorb even a fraction of the story from the point of view of the vanquished, but proudly unbowed. For me, an Indian from another colonized and forcibly "civilized" people, their story has a special resonance. I shall share some of it with you in the chapters ahead. So come, join me on the red road. Mayhap it will inspire some to delve a little into their truly extraordinary, but relatively little known, and often distorted, saga.

Tulsa Airport is small and functional, reminding me of a slightly larger version of the old Muscat airport, in Oman – except Tulsa has aerobridges! Under beautiful clear, blue skies, at a pleasant 28 Celsius, in the taxi on the short but expensive ride from the Airport to the downtown Avis office, I learn the correct pronunciation of my first Native word – they pronounce Tahlequah 'Talaquoa'. The Avis office, a little red-roofed cottage, hunches incongruously amid towering skyscrapers, like a little grey-haired granny lost in Manhattan. The helpful lady at the counter turns out to be a Hunkpapa from the Standing Rock Reservation in North Dakota, the people of Chief Sitting Bull. On hearing my plans to visit the Pine Ridge Reservation, where she had lived at one time, she warns me it is a very rough place with a lot of drunk driving, and that I should definitely not venture out at night. In fact, even during the day, preferably not alone.

Then, after a pause, "I should not be saying this because they are also our people, after all."

She had moved to Tulsa to start a new life after "something very bad happened to me" at Pine Ridge. Bemused but undeterred by this rather alarming early warning, I slide into the neat silver Ford Focus she offers me and set about installing my brand-new Garmin GPS (which I still did not know how to operate). Eventually sorting myself out after a technology tussle, I head out – promptly turning the wrong way! How anyone can do that, with a Garmin screaming out the correct route, is a profound mystery, even to me! I chalk it up to the exhilaration of the moment.

In my little Ford Focus, my trusty Avis steed for the next one month, I hit the open road. I am now in the Central Time Zone, two hours ahead of San Francisco time. It is 2.30 pm as I drive onto US-75, and only then do I realize that, in my childish excitement, I have forgotten all about lunch. It looks like I will just have to make it an early 'lunner' in Tahlequah, as I don't expect to find any watering holes along the freeway. Never mind. It will take less than two hours to cover the 70 miles (113 kms). Excitement trumps hunger!

Bypassing the urban sprawl of Tulsa, I get my first faint whiff of the West, in the name of a passing town, Broken Arrow. From US-51, I drift onto US-351, the Broken Arrow Expressway somewhere becoming the Muskogee Turnpike, and after a while, with a sharp left near the town of Coweta, somehow back onto US-51. I pass the picturesque little settlement of Wagoner, seemingly a very Wild West, one-horse-town sort of place. The hop over little Fort Gibson Lake looks prettier on the map than it does on the ground. My notes shout, "Avoid turnpikes – tolls!" Since Google Maps has a specific option to avoid toll routes, I had figured they must be horrible, expensive ogres, preying on the unwary motorist. Not yet having figured out the intricacies of Garmin, I find myself routed straight onto the Cherokee Turnpike! It turns out to be a joy to drive, and the cost a nominal $1.75, a pleasant surprise for at least this unwary motorist. The passing countryside is green and beautiful, with many flower nurseries – one inviting, "Stop and peek at our bloomers." The ride is only slightly marred by a mysterious, intermittent beep from my Garmin, the reason for which I just cannot figure out. It would be weeks later that I would discover it had been warning me of speed limits and sharp bends in the road!

I am approaching Tahlequah, the Capital of the Cherokee Nation and the end-point of the inhuman Trail of Tears inflicted on them. Authored by the slave-owning, slave-trading President Andrew Jackson, the Indian Removal Act of 1830, at the casual stroke of an uncaring pen, forced the entire Cherokee Nation, from Georgia and eight other eastern States, to abandon everything they owned in the world and suffer a hushed flight through deep snow and winter storms, many barefoot and ill-clad, the four-month, 800-mile death march to distant Tahlequah. As General Andrew Jackson, at the Battle of Horseshoe Bend in the War of 1812, his life was heroically saved by a Cherokee warrior, Junaluska. In the tradition of the Pilgrims treatment of their Wampanoag benefactors, he repaid the Cherokee with the Trail of Tears.

They tried hard, and sincerely, to adopt the ways of the white settlers, some even owning slaves and living in plantation houses, including the famous Trail of Tears Chief, John Ross. Overnight, the Cherokee lost everything except what they could carry on their backs. Much of even that had to be abandoned along the way, over the bitter weeks ahead. All their homes, lands and property were summarily commandeered, without compensation or warning. It was, essentially, grand larceny authorized by the State.

One in four Cherokees, estimated between 2000 and 5000 people, died of cold, hunger, exhaustion and European diseases against which they had no immunity, a numbing, sere tragedy. It was, in reality, the largest massacre of Natives ever. They arrived in Tahlequah largely without their elderly or their children, who died en route; they arrived, essentially, without a past or a future.

As Missionary David Butrick observed, "The government might more mercifully have put to death everyone under a year, or over sixty; rather it had chosen a most expensive and painful way of exterminating these people."

The Government paid unscrupulous contractors $0.56 per head per day, and even on this pittance, they openly cheated, frequently with the connivance of Army supply officers, on both the quality and the quantity of food supplied on that long, pitiless trudge. It outraged even some escorting soldiers.

The prevalent mindset shows in General Sherman's cold-blooded comment, "The more Indians we kill this year, the fewer we will need to kill the next."

Though Justice Marshall, of the US Supreme Court, ruled that Georgia had no right to evict the Cherokee, President Jackson refused to enforce his order, boasting shamelessly, "Marshall has made his decision, now let him enforce it."

Instead, he sent Federal troops to support the action – an object lesson for the ages in the abuse of power. Today, the Cherokee Nation owns less than 0.3% of their original lands, the reward for trying to live in peace and harmony with the invaders. Before the Dawes Act of Massachusetts Senator Henry Dawes, Natives held about 138 million acres. After the Act, it instantly shrank to 48 million acres, with the rest declared "surplus" and, predictably, gifted to European settlers. Those "surplus" acres, again unsurprisingly, just happened to be the best ones.

The Dawes Act, coupled with the 1862 Homestead Act which gifted those prime acres to white settlers, had the deeply pernicious effect of breaking up the Native Nations' long tradition of communal ownership of land, destroying not only their unity but, in the long run, even their ingrained generosity and spirit of sharing for the commonweal.

At the Econolodge, the rather better than usual rooms attest to its recent downgrade from a Comfort Inn. An entire electrical socket separates from the wall when I try to unplug the coffeemaker, hinting at the reason. Eric, the Cherokee/Pawnee Receptionist chats with me about growing up in Tahlequah, and hearing tales of the Trail of Tears from his grandmother. She recalled their moving around Tahlequah on horses, if they were lucky enough to own one. I am hungry to hear more, but Eric does not have many memories of his people.

Finally, I ask Eric to recommend a restaurant nearby. His two both turn out to have closed months ago! The owner suggests another, advising me to drive across to it. Stepping into the gathering dusk, I take a deep breath of the bracing cold air, and right there, less than a hundred meters away, is the restaurant in question! In America, four wheels always win out over two shanks.

I am puzzled. Whereas in most of the world, I could say "thank you", "I agree", or even a simple "yes," in America should it be pistol fingers firing at you, or "ya bet", or "gotcha", or, my all-time favorite, "I hear ya". To me, that last one always seems to be the first half of "but I don't believe ya" or "but I don't understand ya" or "ya stupid foreign nutter"!

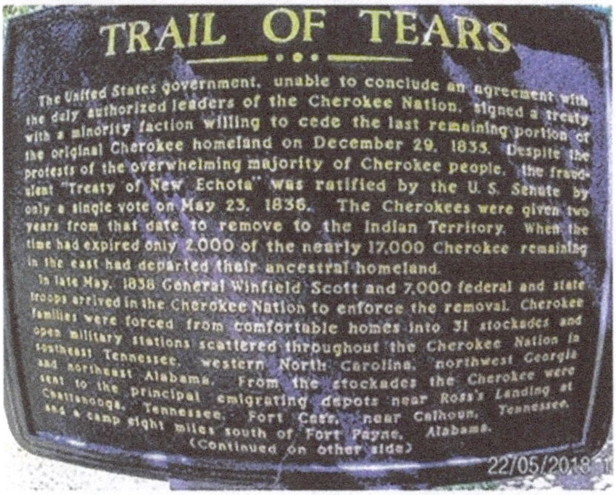

Clockwise from top left: Cherokee National Museum, Tahlequah; sculpture at the Cherokee National Museum; downtown Tahlequah, capital of the Cherokee Nation; Trail of Tears historical marker.

Clockwise from top: Remains of Fort Gibson; USS Batfish at the Muskogee War Memorial; grave of Geronimo, outside Fort Sill; commemorative of Chisholm Trail cattle drives, Duncan.

DAY 2: 22 MAY - TRAIL OF TEARS

A grief-maddened mother desperately reaches back towards the stone cairn under which her small child is buried, while her heartbroken husband tries to gently urge her away. The soldiers will not let them tarry, even to grieve, and their only consolation is the stark knowledge that they, too, will almost certainly join their child in the next few days. This heart-rending sculpture, in the somber Trail of Tears diorama at the Cherokee Heritage Museum, is the searing image branded into my brain, my gut-wrenching memento of Tahlequah. On display at the Museum, the very few surviving, pitiful remnants of the rags and thin moccasins the Cherokee had, in which to trudge the long death road, recall images from Auschwitz. This was no less a genocide. As one Confederate Colonel wrote, "I fought through the Civil War and have seen men shot to pieces and slaughtered by the thousands, but the Cherokee removal was the cruellest work I ever knew."

The Cherokee experience depicted here devastated seven Native Nations, part of State policy to corral, and then force them to distant, climatically alien, and usually unhealthy, infertile areas, where they inevitably sickened and frequently died. The Reservations were, as General Sherman once admitted, places "where Indians live, surrounded by thieves." They herded the Cherokee out of Georgia and eight other eastern States to make the 95th Meridian the border of "Indian Territory". But, with the riptide of Western expansion, the Meridian developed a habit of continually sliding westward. Even Reservation lands shrank or moved altogether if they did not suit the settlers' changing needs, treaties be damned.

As the infamous General Sherman put it, with distilled cynicism, "...treaties were never made to be kept, but to serve a present purpose, to settle a present difficulty in the easiest manner possible, to acquire a desired good with the least possible compensation and then to disregard as soon as the purpose was attained and we were strong enough to enforce a new and more profitable arrangement."

This led one Chief to tell a Congressional Committee, "I think you had better put the Indians on wheels, and you can run them about whenever you wish."

Herded like cattle into roofless stockades by the US Army, it deprived them of even basic human necessities. The refugees were frequently abused by soldiers, though a rare few were appalled and outraged. Meanwhile, white settlers made a wild grab for all their properties, some not hesitating to rob even Native graves in search of valuables. Georgia had already begun the process earlier, by legislating not only against Indians digging for gold but also preventing their testifying against whites in Court. The parallels to Nazism are unavoidable.

The Indian Removal Act of 1830 was the most infamous act of the most infamous, unethical, and extraordinarily avaricious President in US history, Andrew Jackson. It reflected the prevailing views of the time, summed up in a stark statement by a US District Attorney, in the 1879 case of Standing Bear vs. Crook that Natives were "not persons within the meaning of the law."

Their misery did not end with the Trail of Tears (Nunna daul Tsunyi in Cherokee, meaning "the trail where we cried"). As with many tribes across the Plains, over the years to come, most of their children were then forcibly removed to completely alien, European boarding schools run by Christian missionaries, frequently Jesuits. The most notorious was in faraway Carlisle, Pennsylvania, founded by a Captain (later General) Richard Pratt, who expounded the pernicious doctrine, "Kill the Indian; save the Man." Over 175 graves of Native children at the Carlyle School, many marked

"Unknown" as the pious Churchmen had not even bothered to learn their names, bears mute testimony to sheer inhumanity, all in the name of civilization and God. Over the years, more than half the children forced to attend these Christian boarding schools died through disease, malnutrition, abuse, and suicide. The Church, well aware of the situation, looked the other way. As Thomas King asks in his eminently readable "The Inconvenient Indian," would it have been the same if the children had been white? The 1819 legislation for this was called, typically, the Civilization Fund Act. It brings to mind the experience of Australian aborigine children, so poignantly filmed in "Rabbit-Proof Fence".

Not only were the children severely punished for speaking their own language, or holding on to any aspect of their culture, however minor, but by 1902 a Government order decreed they could no longer even wear their prized long hair, as it was "impeding the advancement they are making in civilization."

These children, the future generations of their Native Nations, were being cynically reprogrammed. Every day it was relentlessly drummed into their impressionable minds that their tradition was that of the Devil and that they were all spawns of Evil. Only the Black Coats (missionaries) could save them from the most terrifying and horrific of fates. Violently uprooted spiritually, it is small wonder that over fifty of these traumatized little children were driven to commit suicide, while most others ended up with generations of trauma that psychologists have evidenced in their DNA even today. What Thomas King calls the "unexamined confidence in Western civilization and the unwarranted certainty of Christianity" is frequently at the root of the epidemic of substance abuse and suicide rampant on the Reservations today, though many non-Native scholars dismiss this stark, and undeniable, causality.

Among the most pernicious to come among the Natives were Christian missionaries such as the Reverend Samuel Dutton Hinman who unashamedly advocated less land and more Christianity for the Natives, while helping himself freely to their best acres – all in the name of his God. The Franciscans, in California, actively enslaved Natives for use as forced labor and as servants. The Church's ludicrous condescension to "our Indian wards" concealed a pernicious blend of desire and doctrine. The priests authoritatively proclaimed, "The Church is the Bride of Christ, and she is without error." The endless stream of scandal emanating from that Church, over the years up to the present, questions that arrogant dogma. Only as late as 1978 did the Indian Child Welfare Act finally stop these abuses.

The magnitude of the misery unleashed by a faraway, unheeding, uncaring Administration, blinded by newly discovered gold in Georgia (which no Native had ever objected to their taking anyway, as it had no value to them), was carefully kept from the American public, a Government trepidation that proves morality was far from dead in the average American of the day. This, perhaps, explains why I found the bulk of visitors to the Museum sensitive, caring white Americans, obviously mortified by past inhumanity.

On the flip side of the coin, close to Tahlequah, the extraordinary Sequoia created the Cherokee syllabary, the first of any Native Nation. This achievement led to almost instant literacy across the Cherokee Nation.

Unlike white slave-owners, reports show that the Natives usually treated their slaves well and frequently absorbed them into the family. Later, in 1890, when the controversial Dawes Roll was drawn up, naming each member of the Cherokee Nation, a separate Freedmen's Roll was also created. And this has led to a curious modern-day situation, as I read in the 190-year-old "Cherokee Phoenix" newspaper, founded by Sequoia himself, over lunch on Main Street (the best pizza I have ever tasted though, in the capital of the Cherokee Nation, I could not find a single restaurant serving Cherokee food).

There is a raging controversy among Cherokees today about whether freed slaves are entitled to citizenship of the Cherokee Nation. This issue of granting tribal membership only to full-bloods is what their four-term Principal Chief, Chad Corntassel Smith, campaigned against and lost. Ironically, the concept of blood-based membership of tribes is alien to them, brought to the Natives by the colonizers. And, to complicate matters, the newspaper reported that global political cancer, the fight by elected leaders to extend their terms in power and their electoral base by enrolling more members, many of dubious authenticity. It seems, in more ways than one, the Cherokee has assimilated!

My day had dawned on another beaming Oklahoma morning. Trying to shower, it reminded me why this motel was downgraded, as I had to get help to figure out how to even turn it on, the knob was so well disguised! Breakfast was barely adequate to keep body and soul together, and I silently sympathized with the American guests who have somewhat healthier appetites than mine. The beverage dispenser, too, was out of order. Not too bothered, I notched up a win for diabetes-control instead!

After my searing visit to the Cherokee National Museum (so much more impactful than the presentation at the vaunted Smithsonian), I took some time to tour a mock-up of an ancient Cherokee village on the grounds of the Museum, with circular mud and straw houses, Native games areas (lacrosse was originally a Native sport, nicknamed "the brother of war"), and live demonstrations of archery, beading, and basket-weaving. Our knowledgeable and friendly guide was a Cherokee, but like so many Cherokees today, his features and coloring did not differ from Caucasians.

The mild half-hour was a welcome pause for emotional breath, and I felt in better shape to head out to see the home of the Trail of Tears Chief, John Ross whose wife died on the Trail of Tears. A small, pretty cottage, located somewhat out of town on a little hillock, I arrived to find it locked, despite it being well past its advertised opening hour. Not one to be deterred by such minor inconveniences, I phoned around till I found someone willing to come over and open it up for me. The kindly gentleman finally showed up, and I quickly toured the tiny home. There were a few period displays but, again, it is evident to me just how lightly Natives tread the Earth in terms of the artifacts they leave behind. Ross had led the opposition to Colonel Tom Ridge, the stooge set up by

President Jackson to illegally sign away Cherokee lands under the New Echota Treaty, despite having absolutely no authority to do so.

Heading back into town along the hillocky strip of asphalt, like the farewell wave of a friendly hand, almost before I realized it I arrived at the Murrell House, the only authentic antebellum plantation house in Oklahoma. A prosperous businessman, Murrell had married into a prominent Cherokee family and wholeheartedly threw in his lot with them, including joining their Trail of Tears exodus. Inside the house, the original layout and furnishings have been carefully preserved, while the grounds outside have several low, wood-frame outhouses. The staff was friendly and helpful, despite being inundated by a tsunami of excited children pouring out of the bus of a nearby Native American school. Driving here, from Chief John Ross' home, I am struck by many similar outhouse-type structures along the road, all at least a century old but still in use as regular homes of the locals. It is almost a time warp.

I was due to meet Lisa Snell, the Cherokee Editor of, then, the "Native American Times", and now of "Native Oklahoma", in the town center in the afternoon, and so use the time to explore Tahlequah thoroughly. That took all of fifteen minutes! It is a tiny, charming town with just one real street. Under the mid-day sun, it had a deeply relaxed, 'siesta' atmosphere and neither man nor beast stirred if they could help it. The very sparse traffic made it a parking delight. When I bestirred someone into a conversation, I found the Cherokee friendly, helpful and, unlike most other Native tribes, quite willing to share their story.

After a delicious lunch (still, no Native foods anywhere), I was so relaxed I almost fell asleep in my chair. Eventually, I ambled drowsily over to Drip, a coffee shop so devoted to the arcane art of creating the perfect brew that it is worthy of the hip, yuppie joints of San Francisco. Over some of the best coffee I have ever tasted, even in this coffee-crazy nation, Lisa answered my flood of questions with immense patience, kindness, and good humor. It provided me with an enlightening insight into the contemporary Cherokee Nation.

As I had already noticed, with surprise, many Cherokees look utterly Caucasian. James Wilson, in "The Earth Shall Weep" could have been summing up my reaction, "For someone whose only image of the 'Indian' is still some furred, feathered and beaded figure staring inscrutably out of a nineteenth century photograph, they seem unsettlingly inauthentic and unclassifiable." Cherokees have intermarried extensively with white Americans and full-blooded Cherokee are scarce, and getting scarcer. Due primarily to political expediency, tribal registration today accepts those with as little as one-sixteenth Cherokee blood, or sometimes even less. Usually, it is necessary to prove one of your ancestor's names was on the Dawes Roll.

Lisa reflects meditatively, "I personally believe that we Cherokee are honor-bound to the treaty which made Freedmen tribal citizens. There is a difference, of course, in being Cherokee by blood versus Cherokee by citizenship. Citizenship is a legal and political status. It granted Freedmen that by treaty with the US. "

Tribal membership becomes even more contentious when one takes into consideration this Freedmen's Roll, the list of erstwhile African American slaves.

"Slaves who spoke Cherokee and lived a Cherokee lifestyle were considered to be Cherokee and part of the tribe. I myself have relations whose ancestors owned black slaves on plantations," Lisa confirms.

She is sad at their loss of heritage, "In my own family, my great grandparents were the last Cherokee speakers. Without your language, you lose your culture."

With my children largely strangers to their Bengali mother tongue, I empathize. For the Natives, this has been the hugely damaging, pan-generational legacy of the missionary boarding schools. Looking back, she is distressed she could not receive their tribal heritage from her grandparents in the traditional manner. However, this has not stood in the way of a major resurgence of interest in their Cherokee heritage and ancestry among young adults and teens. The most obvious signs of this resurgence are in Cherokee arts and crafts, in the pride that shines through when they discuss their identity. A Cherokee Nation brochure explains, "One will not hear the anguished voice of a forgotten and broken people. Instead one might hear the pride of a people who faced overwhelming adversity and persisted."

There is little sense of alienation, and their dual heritage sits fairly comfortably on them. As children have become more aware of it, they have become prouder of their Cherokee roots. This becomes diluted the further away they get from a community of full-bloods. The ongoing cultural appropriation by the mainstream has unleashed a bit of "more Indian than thou" in the community.

Lisa laughs lightly, "In the current climate, I think I am prouder to be Cherokee than American!"

An apocryphal story about modern Cherokees tells of then Cherokee Nation Chief, Wilma Mankiller, being asked by a tourist, "Where are all the Indians?"

Her laconic response, "Probably down at Walmart, like everyone else."

The mainstream needs to see them not as historical curiosities, but as regular joes just like us, despite the creation of an American social infrastructure that marginalized their presence. A modern Native leader, Suzan Shown Harjo confirms, "People always think about Indians in the past tense."

Another, Lauren Bomellyn, sum it eloquently, " We're vapors, we're ghosts."

I turn to the matter of spirituality and query her on the many Native Americans who are still Christians today, despite the abuses of the Church and their ancestors having been all but forced to convert away from their own, very deep and very different concept of divinity. They had no equivalent for the idea of communal sin, an inherited curse that turns the world into a hostile place. Theirs was a sunnier divinity.

She mulls the question and confirms, "Chaotic as the world is today, more and more of our people are tending to look back at their traditional religion."

Later in my journey, I would see stark evidence of this on the Pine Ridge Reservation, where more and more churches are empty and some are abandoned, the subject of Mark St. Pierre's haunting film, "Who Will Bury the Dead", which I had the privilege of watching with the film-maker himself.

"There is discrimination everywhere, even in tribal healthcare. You will find blue-eyed, blond-haired people, with just a drop of Native blood, lining up at the free Indian clinics. And they get the same, or frequently better, healthcare than the identifiably Native person sitting next to them who might, perhaps, even be a full-blood Cherokee. There are long waits to see a doctor. We are being given socialized medicine. Understandably, there is growing resentment against half-bloods, because of all this discrimination," she muses.

As Lisa explains, tribal colleges, too, suffer badly from lack of funding. The US Government is Treaty-bound to provide financial support, but, more often than not, pays only lip-service.

She concludes, "I think they just hope the 'problem' will quietly go away."

James Wilson explains this attitude, "...like layers of calloused skin built up over a raw nerve, still effectively distance America from the fact that it grew to greatness by dispossessing and almost exterminating another people."

The Cherokee Nation is among the most prosperous of the tribes now, with myriad commercial ventures, not just casinos. Their economic contribution to Oklahoma is over $2 billion a year. Lisa feels geography has a lot to do with this, being positioned as they are near the central crossroads of the country, on productive land. The Navajo have far more land, but it is isolated and relatively barren. The other eye-opening fact I gleaned from Lisa is that the Cherokee, the largest tribe, with a population of over 505,000, have no Reservation at all, but instead control 14 counties within Oklahoma as the Cherokee Nation.

About this anomaly, Lisa chuckles, "We had good Cherokee lawyers."

While anyone can live and work in the Cherokee Nation, a curious legal dichotomy means that only Natives are subject to tribal law and all others to State law. Not being a Reservation, they are subject to income tax. Lose some, gain some. But in the final analysis, it seems to have turned out to be a definite advantage for the Cherokee.

As we parted, I asked Lisa why, after so much negative history, so many Native Americans joined the US Army, their erstwhile enemy, and fought in all its 20th & 21st Century wars. In fact, as a proportion of their population, more Native Americans serve in the US Armed Forces than any other ethnic group.

She smiled gently, "Remember, it is really their own land that they are fighting for. Also, the Army provided employment."

Later, a Lakota Vietnam Veteran gave me a less optimistic reason – the draft.

"It was either Vietnam or jail. I chose Vietnam," he told me bluntly.

A little known gem is that a Native Pima, Ira Hayes, was one of the Marines who raised the US flag at Iwo Jima, immortalized in the iconic photograph by Joe Rosenthal in 1945.

With my heart battered by the Museum in the morning, and my head buzzing with Lisa's insights in the afternoon, I drive down Main Street. What a blissful experience - a town with so little traffic and street parking that is plentiful and free! Little Mom-and-Pop stores dot one side of the street, and pretty, leafy parks snooze on the other. There is not much to Tahlequah beyond Main Street, but what there is, is ... peaceful!

Today, the Cherokee Nation is a self-governing entity with its own laws and institutions, based at the Cherokee Nation Capital in Tahlequah. Though they are relatively better off than the other Nations, their language, a key anchor for any culture, has been nearly eradicated by the concerted "civilizing" State Policy of the past. As former Principal Chief, Chad Corntassel Smith, put it, "As important as growing our economic self-reliance, I believe, is the need to preserve, and indeed propagate, our Cherokee language and culture. For me, these have been among the main pillars of community development, across all my terms in office."

As I pass the flourishing Cherokee-owned casinos, hotels, and film studios on my way to my Motel, I see reasons for optimism about the future peeping through. Battered and decimated by the merciless Trail of Tears, and culturally amputated by the concerted repression of the victors, the once numerous Cherokees are finally beginning to recover. Despite the horrors of the past, there is an air of cautious optimism. Tomorrow will be another day!

It has been a fascinating - and emotional - day, and I am happy to return to my Motel, to contemplate. It has also been a good day to be a Senior, with discounts everywhere! Now, I need to prepare for tomorrow when I face the first of my more daunting 6-hour drives. On to fresh fields and pastures new – literally so, as it would turn out!

DAY 3: 23 MAY - LANDLOCKED SUBMARINE

A hulking, honest-to-goodness World War II submarine, lazing in the dry, grassy, landlocked heart of the Continent! It was a surreal sight that greeted me on this slight diversion from my Native American pilgrimage. I found it, despite being a bit misguided by my hitherto reliable Garmin.

The USS Batfish is a Balao-class submarine, famed for sinking three Japanese submarines in 1945. Inside, though expected, it still feels alarmingly cramped and claustrophobic, with the crews' beds slung directly beneath deadly torpedoes. Decommissioned in 1969, it now slumbers peacefully in the War Memorial Park at Muskogee, Oklahoma. How the war-weary submarine moved all the way from the ocean, at New Orleans, to Muskogee, is a saga in itself – but that is a tale for another day. Most poignant are the three long rows of simple podiums, each commemorating a US submarine sunk during World War II. In one corner lies a large, rusted, metal fragment of the USS Oklahoma, sunk at Pearl Harbour and now a permanent memorial, shimmering like a ghost just below the surface of the water. At the Visitor Centre, a display of huge naval guns has become a jungle gym by a group of excited, small children – death-dealing monsters transformed into joyous playthings for the innocent.

Encouraged by the beautiful roads, I ignored my own caution against toll roads and headed onto the H.E. Bailey Turnpike, which is also US-44. Escorted by lush greenery on both sides and the occasional raindrops, I was on my way to Lawton, home of the famous and greatly feared Comanche. Driving out of Tahlequah bright and early, I passed "Coffee Hollow Drive". Yearning for my missed caffeine boost at breakfast, I interpreted the speed limit with a certain flexibility. Almost immediately, I passed a sign to "Correctional Facility." Thereafter, another pointed to "Cemetery." I eased off the accelerator.

Along the way, I gazed with amazement at the sight of a giant semi-trailer run accidentally right off the road and into the roadside ditch, by a little red Honda sedan loaded with hysterical teenage girls. Size is not everything!

My next stop is historic Fort Gibson, close to the landlocked submarine. I arrived early and had to wait a while for staff to arrive, after which I helped them open up the place. The Visitor Centre video was a pleasant surprise in its fair and even-handed take on history. As literature explains, "It guarded the American frontier, in Indian Territory, from 1824 until 1888." Unlike many garrisons on the Frontier, this was an open fort without an enclosed stockade, comprising a collection of unexpectedly small buildings. The only ones that remain are those made of stone; the rest have disappeared with the ebbing tide of history and weather. Rolling green hills mottled with trees, and small undulating meadows surround the Fort. I found my first reference to "Indian Territory" on the foundation marker here. Further down the road, a large wooden stockade, complete with medieval-looking stocks for the naughty, offers a glimpse into the cramped, primitive living conditions of the time.

When built, it was the furthest Western point reached by white settlers. For half a century, it was a genuine peacemaker, unlike Samuel Colt's creation. Fort Gibson even claimed the remarkable distinction of bringing peace to the inveterate enemies, the Osage, and the Cherokee. It also garrisoned both the American-Mexican war for Texas and the infamous Trail of Tears. Despite its less–than–exciting history, it hosted several famous residents over the years

– Robert E Lee, Zachary Taylor, Jefferson Davis, and Nathan Boone, son of the storied Daniel Boone.

By the 1850s, though, the Cherokee were bitterly complaining about the liquor and brothels at Fort Gibson destroying their people and demanding its closure. Most unusually, the Army acceded to their request, shut down the Fort in 1857 and, even more unusually, handed over the keys to the Cherokee Nation, who did ***not*** burn it down! If nothing else, Fort Gibson proved, with silent eloquence, that peaceful coexistence was always possible.

The remains of the Fort, other than the recreated stockade, are small and sparse. For a place with such a story, it disappoints just a little. As I drove off, I noticed an intriguing location marked on my map, "The Castle of Muskogee". Unfortunately, I did not have the time for a detour today, to explore that medieval-sounding mystery.

Located up a lovely, winding road atop a leafy hill sits the Museum of the Five Civilized Tribes. I was desperate with curiosity to find out just why they were the 'civilized tribes.' Were the others not? They comprise the Cherokee, Choctaw, Chickasaw, Creek and Seminole tribes, every one of which suffered the Trail of Tears, a sadly ironic fate for the civilized. Tellingly, the reservation thrust upon the Chickasaw and Choctaw was known as Boggy Depot.

A Museum official, Sarah Little Feather, laughed at my breathless query, "We were the settled tribes; farming, living in permanent houses, in static villages, with a structured tribal government. So, I suppose, the Europeans of that time considered us 'civilized'. I guess no one has felt it necessary to change the name since."

The Museum itself is lamentably scant, with few exhibits worth the trip. It is more contemporary art gallery than a museum. Like Fort Gibson, for such celebrated tribes, this is a poor offering. As I wandered disconsolately around the sparse gallery, I bumped into Eric Standing Bear, a young Creek artist whose work is on display. I asked him about young Creeks in the modern age.

With a straight face he replied, "These days, we scalp fewer enemies and do less of the smoke signals, war-paint, and Tonto stuff."

Then, thoughtfully, "The US Government has always wanted to 'destroy the Indian and – perhaps – save the man.' I guess they succeeded. Assimilation is, sort of, complete, be it good or bad."

As the old Native American saying succinctly puts it, "Only the earth endures."

I left in a "vacant and pensive mood," pondering the tectonic interaction of civilizations, and demographic shifts. However, my pathetically un-philosophical stomach reminded me of more down-to-earth matters – lunch. I had a long 425-kilometer drive ahead, through the afternoon, and I know of few more efficient fuels for the soul than a juicy, Oklahoma steak, especially since, here too, no eatery serves any Native food! I needed to make a refueling stop for my car too, I realized.

As I drove into a nearby 'gas' station, I was faced with another learning experience. Spoilt as we are in Oman and India with full-service pumps, I had never experienced self-service before! It took me a little while, and a few missteps, to figure out just how it works, and fill my car's nearly empty tank. My little Ford had a big thirst! With the car's tank fed, I took care of my human tank and settled in for the long haul. The gradual transition from the more rural eastern Oklahoma to the urban central areas was marked by a change from a two-lane to a three-lane interstate, more traffic, some inevitable deterioration in road courtesy, the appearance of an occasional Police cruiser, and a substantial decline in windscreen insect splatter.

The Oklahoma Turnpikes are beautiful and it is easy to understand why the Great American Road-trip is such an integral part of life in this country. Unfortunately, this time, the toll machine refused to accept my money, in some mysterious sulk. The disembodied Help voice advised me to just drive through and then report it to the toll authority later. The moment I did, to my utter consternation, it set off a blaring klaxon! With panicked visions of SWAT troopers suddenly swooping down on me, I pulled over without further ado and called them, to sort it out. The blasé, easy-going response of the helpful operator was rather an anti-climax, after the drama of the jangling alarm. Enough excitement for today!

My research had shown that Fort Sill, at Lawton, being an operating military installation, requires an Entry Pass to get in and, from their unenlightening website, getting one seemed to involve both time and a cumbersome background check. So, I decided to apply for one at the Fort's Visitor Control Centre before heading to my Motel, hoping to save time by collecting it the next morning. It was grating to discover the main road named after General Sheridan, the man who sullied the reputation of the US Army with his less than scrupulous handling of the wars with the Natives of these Great Plains.

Blindly following my Garmin's directions suddenly confronted with a heavily chained and bolted gate, instead of the welcoming entrance to Fort Sill that I expected. Was temporary insanity afflicting my beloved Garmin? After several false starts, I finally located the place, only to discover that I had inadvertently arrived on the day of the graduation of the military cadets. The crush of visiting friends and family, all waiting to apply for their Entry Passes, spilled out in all directions. As I wearily made my way from the car park, a lady noticed the Illinois plates on my little Ford and excitedly asked how long it had taken me to drive all the way. Learning I had come from just "down the road," Tulsa, was a disappointment.

It took over 45 minutes in the queue for me to reach the counter. Once there, a helpful officer had me processed and my Pass issued within minutes. I would not have to return tomorrow. It turned out to be a far easier and pleasanter experience than the unwelcoming website had led me to expect. Fort Sill believes in managing expectations, I guess. In true bureaucratic style, on the Entry Pass, I was an authorized "Gues" and my "Assigned Escor" was my Passport! It gave me till 23:59 hours the next day to explore the tiny Fort Sill Museum.

Finally, on my way to the Relax Inn Motel, I stopped for a quick dinner, knowing there would be none available there. As usual, the daunting portion sizes intimidated me. Their definition of "small" (or "regular" as their marketers prefer, since "small" apparently does not exist in the American vocabulary) does not square with the Oxford English Dictionary! Completely satiated with just a quarter of my meal, I doggy-bagged the rest, for my next two meals, and perhaps even three. America, the bountiful!

It had been a long, exhausting drive to cover the 262 miles (425 kilometers) from Tahlequah to Lawton, and I was looking forward to a hot shower and bed. Walking into the Motel, I found, sure enough, another Raj from Gujarat in India, in charge. He was friendly, though the room turned out barely acceptable, with the usual dull, dirty-looking carpeting and poor lighting, which, I guess, hides the carpet from undesirable scrutiny. Though it lacked some basic amenities, such as a room telephone and a coffee-maker, I realized gratefully that even mediocre motels in America have excellent, free wi-fi everywhere. I would have no difficulty getting my column off to the "Muscat Daily" in Oman.

DAY 4: 24 MAY - COMANCHE ATTACK!

"Comanche attack!"
The dread alarm was very familiar to Frontiersmen, regularly fed fantastical stories of ferocious attacks by bloodthirsty savages. Universally recognized as the finest horse meisters in the world, the Comanche developed a rare, pure warrior society on the back of this horse culture and, eventually, killed more of the colonizers invading their lands, than any other tribe. However, by the time they made peace in 1875, the proud Comanche had been driven to the brink of extinction, with just 1597 survivors. The invaders exterminated as much as 90% of their Nation, primarily through European diseases. Even today, clawing their way slowly back from the very edge, they still number barely 17,000. I was keen to discover the reality behind the stereotype, as I wandered the streets of little Lawton, the home of the proud Comanche, in southwestern Oklahoma.

At the fascinating little Comanche National Museum, I fell into conversation with the warm, friendly Carney Many Came (an abbreviation of his full Comanche name), their Culture Specialist, a full-blood Comanche. A people-person, he was happy to talk freely and extensively with visitors who are interested and are willing listeners. Since I met both those parameters, in spades, I asked, rather stupidly, if the Comanches are still the finest horse breeders in the world.

"Well, these days, the cities and towns are not really horse-friendly," he grinned tolerantly, "so no, these days all our horsepower is automotive."

In the modern era, the Comanche, along with the Navajo and other tribes, are more famous for their Code Talkers who played such a vital, but till recently unsung, role for the Allies in World War II. I wondered what his people think of the wasicu, the white man (known as "thievo" in Comanche), these days; those who took their lands and destroyed their traditional way of life.

As we strolled along, he smiled, "There are no cuss words in our Native languages. Nor do we have words for owning the land either. Please remember our history goes back centuries and not just when we were overtaken by white people who were more numerous than us."

The Museum reminded me that scalping was unknown to the Natives; it was introduced by the Spaniards and white trader companies to tally Natives killed for bounty. And as for land, "termination" under "eminent domain" (successor to the even more pernicious Manifest Destiny) continued right up to President Eisenhower. The first, and so far only, President to meet with and sympathetically listen to them was President John F. Kennedy, though it had to wait till President Obama for a formal apology to the Native American people for their centuries of mistreatment.

Despite it all, Carney urges acceptance of realities and reconciliation, without losing their unique Comanche identity. This, now tiny, tribe is considered to be exceptionally aware and proud of its identity and heritage. Though over the years, there has been some intermarriage outside the tribe, many of them have been into other Native tribes, rather than to Caucasians. Hence, their bloodlines are less diluted than the Cherokees, though possibly slightly more so than the Lakota. Sadly though, these days, most Comanche, too, do not know their own, almost 5000-year-old Numic language.

As Carney puts it eloquently, "My language is native to this land."

The Comanche Government has tried to encourage its revival, though efforts have been sporadic, depending on the political expediency of the Chief of the moment.

Carney told me about an elderly white couple from Chicago who visited the Museum some months earlier. Having spent a lot of time looking through the exhibits, they were distraught at the misdeeds of their ancestors. It was left to Carney to console them, and advise them to acknowledge and forgive the sins of the past while making the most of the present, a time for reconciliation, acceptance and moving forward.

He had advised them, "Don't beat yourselves up about what they did to Natives. You cannot live in the old West. The old West no longer exists, just as the American Civil War is over. You cannot turn back the hands of time and redo American history."

His forbearance and compassion humbled me. As I was to discover on my journey, this is archetypal of the attitudes of many thinking, decent, white Americans, who are ashamed of the treatment meted out to the Natives by their forebears, and most Native Americans today, who are more forgiving of the sins of yesteryear. This is the brightest shoot of hope, that the country can acknowledge the past and move towards a considerably brighter and more fulfilling future, hand in hand.

Wandering on, I am curious about his perspective of the contemporary Comanche's world.

He is insightful, "My Creator made me a Comanche and I have no desire to be anyone else but Comanche. I can only be who my Creator made me to be, but I can also be an American just like an Italian, a German, a Frenchman, a Spaniard, an Arab, or a Polish man. I believe our young Comanches need to make the most of the opportunities they have today. After all, this Continent is the only home we have ever known."

On their current political status, he explains that not only was the population of their last five remaining bands decimated at the time of their "coming in" (I prefer not to use the word 'surrender', as there never has been anything remotely surrendered, or defeated, in the bearing of these Native Nations), but in the 20th Century, their massive 3-million-acre Treaty Reservation was pulverized by greedy settlers till they are, today, left with just a straggle of disconnected 160-acre tracts of poor, unproductive land, scattered disjointedly about. And even over those shreds, he explains, the Comanche exercise only quasi-sovereignty, as they entirely depend on the whims of an uncaring and ignorant Congress.

It even requires them to part with a significant portion of the revenue from their five casinos to the State Government, though it does little for them in return, and they desperately need the money to better the living conditions of their own people. The large-hearted Carney, predictably, looks at the glass half-full, happy that whatever revenues remain in tribal hands are going a long way to benefit the Comanche.

He points out an unexpected benefit that resulted from the pillaging of their treaty lands, "Discrimination was much worse for Natives in the white border towns which sat just outside the Reservations, especially on the Northern Plains and in the western US. Because of the breakup of the old Comanche Reservation into allotments, in the early 1900s, the white homesteaders intertwined as neighbors next to Comanche, which allowed for dialogue, understanding, and to become acquainted with one another throughout the 20th Century. Comanche were not isolated like Native people on distant Reservations but could interact more with the dominant culture."

Sharing the campus with the much smaller Cherokee National Museum is the inadequate Museum of the Great Plains. Perhaps my expectations had been heightened by my visit to its fascinating little neighbor, but I was frustrated to find little of the history of the Great Plains there and a dearth of meaningful artifacts. My visit was brief.

The Relax Inn Motel room is the sort that encourages guests to stay away as long as possible. My shower had all the enthusiasm and alacrity of a geriatric government filing clerk. Even the servers at the local McDonald, where I breakfasted, looked like customers were bringing utter tragedy to their lives. With such inducements, I headed out to nearby Duncan, enjoying the beautiful weather, across gently undulating hillocks with fields where farmers were, literally, making hay while the sun shines. The freeway was graduated with road-kill instead of mileposts, and then, right in the midst of rural Oklahoma, redolent with the steamy fragrance of cow manure, I passed "Plato Road"!

One of the best of its kind anywhere, the experiential museum at the Chisholm Trail Heritage Centre at Duncan, Oklahoma, is well worth the detour, though I somehow missed the Remingtons they claimed for their Garis Gallery. Outside Hollywood reel-life, and our misguided childhood games, the interaction of real-life cowboys and Native tribes was limited, as the cowboys represented the second wave, after the hardy frontiersmen had already 'settled' the West beyond reversal. I could not help but admire the sheer grit and tenacity of these tough men on the long, hard, very dangerous cattle drives – for which they received a dollar a day, usually for 100 days of fifteen, often literally back-breaking hours, death always lurking just a few sharp horn tips away. In a few days, I will follow that same trail to its railhead at Dodge City. Thankfully, I will do so riding four wheels rather than four hooves, buffeted not by herds of stampeding Longhorns but zephyrs off the utterly empty, lonely plains of Kansas.

After a satisfying lunch at the Lawton Red Lobster, where both the food and the service were excellent, I was back at Fort Sill to spend the afternoon in a frenetic hunt for Geronimo's grave. While the final resting place of the last great Comanche Chief, the mixed-breed (or, as they considered him, Comanche white man) Quanah Parker, is also here, I did not uncover it easily. Curiously, Parker's grave is in the cemetery in the heart of the Fort, while Geronimo's is tucked away in a distant nearly forgotten corner.

A functional Army base, where soldiers from around the world attend artillery training, Fort Sill is a massive, sprawling facility, not at all a fort in the traditional sense. Hardly anything survives of its historic past, and I can testify to how easy it is to get lost within its labyrinth. In good military tradition, the guards at the gates were courteous but had no clue about the grave (almost certainly, not even about whom I was talking), or even some roads within their own Fort. However, knowing I was somewhere in the approximate vicinity of the grave of one of the greatest Native warriors, I was a very determined bloodhound on the scent of a juicy bone I could almost taste, determined to find it even if it took me all night. After all, my Pass gave me till 23:59 to do so. Then, discovering to my alarm the Main Gate firmly locked and bolted, with no alternate directions or contact information, and unable to unearth a single human on the campus, I wandered distractedly into the Fort Kitchen by mistake - and finally received guidance. Between those rather inexact directions, sheer perseverance, and my good, old-fashioned paper map, I finally discovered it!

The last, and probably greatest, war chief of the legendary Apaches sleeps under a simple cairn of rocks amid the graves of his family, far from their beloved Arizona home. This was the man who inspired such fear in the Army that, to receive his surrender with his last 24 warriors, the much-hated General Nelson Miles felt it necessary to send 5000 troops, 500 Apache scouts, a flying column of cavalry and thousands of civilian militias.

The great Geronimo was initially shipped off to the humid, unhealthy swamps of Florida, far from the dry mountain elevations of his native Arizona. When that did not kill him, as the Army had probably hoped, he was permitted to join Pawnee Bill's Wild West Show (where he was advertised as "The worst Indian that ever lived", reportedly to his huge amusement), and then spent his last years at Fort Sill.

Controversy about his apparent conversion to Christianity at 79, shortly before his death, dogged his final years. Some felt the canny warrior joined the Church of President Roosevelt in a vain attempt to persuade him to allow a return to his native Arizona, something that the remnants of his people would be permitted to do only in the mid-20th Century. Others believed Naiche, the son of the legendary Cochise, genuinely converted him. However, at his funeral, that same Naiche savagely criticized Geronimo's failure to accept Christianity. Interestingly, Geronimo's simple cairn of stones has no Christian cross over it, unlike the nearby grave of Chief Nana and his family. Much like politicians, priests too, apparently, did not hesitate to con their God by claiming yet another soul "saved", however dubious the assertion.

The wasicu, white man, always had a genius for material things, while the Natives always had it for the spiritual. In return for their material things, to which it was so easy to become addicted, the wasicu demanded the Natives give up their Great Spirit. The 'black coat' priests insisted, they were the only ones who knew all about the One Big Spirit and that no one else knew anything at all. The Natives were all misguided primitives, living in a sordid world of superstition and evil. It is little wonder that followers of Wakan Tanka, the Great Mystery, the First Principle, the Supreme Spirit, about whom they humbly claimed to know only a little, found them ludicrous and bewildering. Eventually, however, the Jesuits persuaded the US Government to ban all practice of Native religions or beliefs, making the slightest act punishable with ten years in prison plus a devastating $10,000 fine. This onerous law, so contrary to the founding spirit of America itself, was not repealed until as late as 1979.

I lingered awhile by the simple grave, in silent and somber homage – and then return slowly to the 21st Century.

DAY 5: 25 MAY - A MISSING HEAD

Yes, there is definitely a head missing! Actually, on closer inspection, there are, at least, three heads missing – Red Cloud, Sitting Bull, and the greatest of them all, Crazy Horse. Anadarko is a town so tiny that it is literally true, if you blink, you will miss it. Elsewhere in the world, it would be a village. Its claim to fame is that it hosts the Hall of Fame of Native Americans. In a quiet, bucolic little park sit rows of beautifully sculpted busts representing centuries of tempestuous leadership. The Visitor Center did not open at 9 am as advertised but, since all the sculptures are outdoors, along a long, narrow, asphalted walk, skirting a central dew-dappled, grassy field, it did not matter. All the usual suspects were there – Sequoia,

Sacajawea, Pocahontas, Cochise, Geronimo, et al, but, for some unfathomable reason, not three of the greatest.

I am dumbfounded to discover that one of them, Charles Curtis, became Vice President of the USA, while another, Stand Wattie, was a Confederate general, the very last to surrender. Will Rogers, for whom Oklahoma International Airport (OKE) is named, was the highest-paid actor in Hollywood in the 1930s, though he never played a Native in any of his 50+ movies. Ely Parker, a Seneca, wrote the Terms of Surrender for Ulysses Grant, at Appomattox, at the end of the Civil War. His penmanship was the best of them all. These are all modern American achievements that one rarely associates with Native Americans. I had made an early start, to take in tiny Anadarko and was rewarded with enlightenment.

A tad down the same road is the Southern Plains Indian Museum but, before I could look for it, I found myself well past the entire town of Anadarko, and back amidst the endless fields. Ah well, something for another time, perhaps.

Leaving Lawton, I bid a tearful farewell to my friends, the bedbugs at the Motel. We had become blood-brothers overnight - though they left me with an itch to hit the road early. Knowing he would take suitable care of them, I commended them to Raj from Gujarat and headed off on my trusty metal steed. As I passed Medicine Park on the outskirts of Lawton, I offered a respectful nod towards the grave of the great Geronimo, to the right of I-44. I felt deeply privileged to have been near such greatness, even long dead.

Further down the road, I passed the little town of Boone and wondered if someone named it after Daniel Boone. There was no time to stop and find out – had there been anyone around to find out from. The usual clear blue skies, with nary a stray tornado around, had turned overcast and dark near Anadarko but the lowering clouds cleared as I neared Oklahoma City. Speaking of tornadoes, the Great Plains Museum, in Lawton has a realistic simulation of a tornado shelter with the sounds of one passing overhead – and it is far scarier than any horror movie my wife has ever forced me to watch. Going past El Reno, a prominent yellow sign cheerily advised, "Hitchhikers may be escaping inmates." No lifts for anyone today!

The gently rolling hills and the mesmerizingly undulating ribbon of asphalt stretching over the horizon, with the occasional lonely oil-well phlegmatically ducky-dipping in the middle of nowhere, rather suddenly gave way to flat countryside, the curvaceous road morphing into a dead-straight arrow in the blink of an eye. As the land flattened, the winds picked up, and wind farms with ultra-modern turbines began to appear.

I had entered the Great Plains.

Approaching Oklahoma City through the low prairies woven with silvery-gold tipped Bermuda grass anchored in red earth, I stopped briefly at Yukon to look at a historic marker for an old Chisholm Trail watering hole. An easily-missed spot, it marks a key trail crossing where the herds, and the herders, used to stop for water. A little historical imagination easily turned the surrounding hills of modern concrete back into open fields, with thousands of Longhorns tramping their dusty way into the sunset. Not for the first time, I was grateful for my habit of reading up and preparing for my trips well in advance so as not to miss anything of interest or significance. Regret, on having missed a fascinating nugget out of ignorance is, I believe, a bitter cup.

I finally rolled into Oklahoma City. Its name derives from the Choctaw "ukla" meaning person and "huma" meaning red. Traffic on the freeway was still fairly light and well disciplined. Even entering the city, it remained that way, much to my surprise. Walking into the Rodeway Inn, I found it owned by – you guessed it – a Patel from Gujarat! So, the Patels really do own all the motels in America.

This is a big city with a small-town feel. Though it has all the big city blessings, like expensive parking and impatient drivers, the people are unexpectedly warm and friendly. It is the only major city I have ever visited where busy street intersections have blinking stop lights rather than the regular, intimidating red traffic lights, relying on the self-discipline of motorists to stop in sequence. And they do!

I had read wonderful things about the Red Earth Gallery at the Santa Fe Plaza and so, finding myself in the vicinity, took a stroll through it, even though it was not the month for their great annual festival. The art displayed there was impressive and the small, elongated gallery worth the time I invested in it. A pity the price-tags were eye-watering for the likes of me. Wandering further afield, I discovered the quaint streets of charming Bricktown where, yes, everything is made of brick – the roads, buildings, parks, everything. This seems to be Oklahoma City's fun quarter. Great, as these two are to be my relaxation days. I cannot believe I have been on the road a full week already and completed a quarter of my odyssey.

As usual, the portion sizes of the meals almost reduce me to tears. They will not let me buy a kid's meal instead. O, America! After that stupefying lunch, tonight I will again have to resort to my "Lyallpur Navratan Mixture" for a snack-dinner top-up. Today I have clocked 128 miles (206 kms) in just under three hours of driving. Not a stressful day at all.

Clockwise from top left: Fraser's "End of the Trail"; sculpture outside the National Cowboy & Western Heritage Museum, Oklahoma City; chuckwagon lunch at the Cowboy Museum; the Native American Hall of Fame, Anadarko; historical marker at the site of the "battle" of the Washita; cheery roadside sign in Oklahoma.

Clockwise from top: The eerie silence of the fateful Washita; a beef yard at Dodge City; lonely yesteryear caboose at the Oklahoma Railway Museum; variety show at the Long Branch Saloon, Dodge City; Wyatt Earp still patrols Dodge City.

DAY 6: 26 MAY - REMINGTON AND THE CHUCK-WAGONS

Today was relatively relaxed. The steamy breath of Oklahoma City greeted me with a 35 Celsius morning and a glare factor that would have impressed an Oman summer. It almost felt like home!

The Oklahoma Railway Museum will be of interest to hard-core train buffs, but perhaps less so for just the mildly curious. Volunteer enthusiasts have worked diligently for years to acquire, refurbish and exhibit items from the country's railroad glory days. The rolling stock they have collected is a tribute to their passion. The little spur from the Museum to the main railroad line was a prayerful plea for more exhibits to roll in from somewhere, anywhere.

It is a short drive to the sprawling National Cowboy & Western Heritage Museum, a remarkable place marred only by being narrated solely from the perspective of the "riptide of Western expansion," as Thomas King puts it. The dramatic centerpiece of the Museum is Fraser's towering sculpture, "The End of the Trail," an affront to the Native warrior, portraying him as utterly defeated, destroyed, finished, reflecting the arrant jingoism of the era. Even the warrior's horse is so emaciated and skeletal that it almost amounts to animal cruelty. In reality, even surrendered the bearing of these warriors was invariably proud, unvanquished, unconquerable, despite all adversity.

Where progressive cities, like San Francisco, are removing such condescending commemoratives to less prominent spaces where they can be put into proper historical context for viewers, here this beautifully sculpted paean to imperial hubris still stands front and center. It reminded me of John Marshall's sage observation in his book on Crazy Horse – the universal roots of trouble have always been fear, anger and, above all, arrogance. I was conflicted between the aesthetic and the cultural aspects of Fraser's masterpiece and wondered if, in this far more enlightened day, it really should still be the centerpiece of this beautiful Museum. There are other, equally beautifully sculpted pieces scattered around the Museum that could easily replace this castaway of time. I would especially commend the exquisite 15-foot Gerald Balcair "Canyon Princess," the sculpture of a female cougar.

Even in the paintings of such undisputed masters of the day as Remington and Russell, stunning errors and misconceptions surface. For instance, in the battle regalia of a war chief, in one Remington, his weapons include a stickball stick, used in a Native game, a precursor of lacrosse, not war.

I receive the distinct impression that this otherwise fascinating Museum tacitly propagates the image of colorful, exotic, but ultimately wild and 'uncivilized' Natives, against the heroic and glorious cowboys, settlers, fur trappers, US Cavalry and their ilk. Noble savages they may be, but savages nevertheless. It does seem to reflect either a lack of balance that has not been corrected over the decades or, perhaps more sinisterly, a continuing Goebbels-like indoctrination, more so as a large proportion of local visitors are young, impressionable schoolchildren. Far more moving is Charles Schreyvogel's "The Last Drop", a poignant sculpture of a cowboy offering his last drop of water to his faithful horse– a quiet celebration of true heroism.

An entire gallery is devoted to glorifying Hollywood's portrayal of the West, despite it being largely responsible for the incorrect and demeaning image of the Native American now rooted so firmly in the popular imagination worldwide. An entire wall showcases John

Wayne, the archetypal heroic cowboy. Once again, I was conflicted between my admiration for him as a brilliant, versatile actor and my horror at both his real-life attitude to Native Americans, such as his behavior at Marlon Brando's Oscar award night and the one-sided, one-dimensional propaganda of Manifest Destiny that is manifest in his films.

As if to compensate for this unfair presentation just a little, it was the day of their Chuck-wagon Festival. Because of it, neither my Discount Coupon nor my Senior status prevailed. Despite that slight damper for my wallet, I dug enthusiastically into the traditional fare of the old West, primarily corn, grits and various indeterminate dishes, all uniformly awash in brown gravy. Deftly ignoring the Voice of Diabetes, I sneaked in some of their tempting, sugary desserts too. Though it is designed primarily to entertain and educate young schoolchildren, I found I enjoyed it as much as they so obviously did. It would have been even more enjoyable had the temperature not soared to such Oman-like majesty, necessitating the drinking of many bottles of water – with a corresponding number of visits to the facilities, which involved some considerable effort to locate! My advice for visitors - do not wait till the last minute to search for the loo. It is never where you want it to be!

Various Wild West shows and displays around the campus added to the carnival atmosphere. The best of them was the Annie Oakley shooting demonstration by a sharpshooter couple who have toured the world with their show. Watching her shooting, I was slack-jawed in awe. I know the original Annie Oakley, who figured so prominently in Buffalo Bill's Wild West Show, may have performed a whit better, but probably no more than that. Bravo, Annie of the Museum, even though I cannot now recall your real name.

Today was an easy day, having driven just 34 miles (55 kms). Tomorrow I finally head out of Oklahoma, into the wilds of rural Kansas. On the way, I will stop to pay homage to a place of a heartbreaking tragedy. But that is a tale for the morrow.

DAY 7: 27 MAY - DEATH AT DAWN

"Roses aren't red, Violets aren't blue, All my dreams are dead, I don't know what to do." That cheery ditty on the car radio, heading out on the long slog to Dodge City, set the tone for my first, very somber stop – fateful Washita. Even when I later crossed my first State line into Kansas, the FM still exhorted me to "Rahse to the Oklahoma kahnd aaf lahfe." Under clear blue skies, the temperature inched up from a pleasant 26 Celsius and humidity began to build. On the empty roads, I passed long trailers carrying horses, and I mused on how the times they have indeed been achangin'. Those horses sure have it good, riding mechanical horses instead of being ridden!

As the traffic thinned, and the landscape turned even emptier, a sign pointed off into nowhere claiming to be "Berlin." I am on part of historic Route 66, on which so many have traveled over the decades, from Chicago to Santa Monica in California. The longest driveable stretch of this famous road, 392 miles long, is in Oklahoma. It is littered with cultural appropriations, generally wildly inaccurate. One sign, for the "Cherokee Trading Post," displays an alleged Southern Cherokee wearing a Northern Plains war bonnet, something alien to the Cherokee. On another scale, an Arizona "trading post" boasts "The world's largest tepee" – made of sheet metal! It appears the tradition of simply helping yourself to what belongs to your neighbor, whether or not you understand its value, is still alive and flourishing.

Perhaps it was the lure of the empty roads but I seemed to make a rather fast passage to Dodge, as I reached the Washita a full hour ahead of my schedule. This turned out to be fortunate as it took me much longer than I had expected to hike both the Upper and Lower Trails, through the silent, brooding fields, in the torrid 37 Celsius. It is a testimony to my passion that neither the heat nor the fields awash in poison ivy and rattlesnakes (I have an absolute phobia of all snakes and refuse to believe any might be "harmless" as I am frequently assured!) deterred me from making the slow, contemplative trek across that fateful campsite, my mind's eye visualizing the heartrending scene playing out in all its pitiful tragedy.

Peace Chief Black Kettle of the Southern Cheyenne was an ardent believer in harmony and peaceful coexistence though it cost him dearly in both followers and credibility. As a Peace Chief, his band comprised mainly women, children and the elderly. Almost exactly four years earlier, the great Peace Chief was bringing his people to live under the protection of Fort Lyon, Colorado. Colonel John Chivington instructed him to camp at nearby Sand Creek. While encamped peacefully, Chivington with a force of 700 troops, 4 mountain howitzers and 500 militias, suddenly attacked without warning, resulting in the horrific Sand Creek Massacre of 105 women and children, and 28 old men. A huge American flag and a large white flag were flying over the camp. Chivington's blood-crazed, out-of-control troops did not spare even their own flag. All the dead were scalped and mutilated with incredible cruelty, a horror that is, understandably, not much publicized by the Army.

The National Park Service brochure on the Sand Creek Massacre quotes an 1865 Congressional Joint Committee report, "It is difficult to believe that beings in the form of men, and disgracing the uniform of United States soldiers and officers could commit or countenance...such acts of cruelty and barbarity."

The Chief's few warriors were away hunting. Black Kettle barely escaped while they seriously injured his wife in nine places. Sand Creek triggered, and Washita exacerbated the Great Plains Indian

War. After the massacre, over 3000 warriors joined the Teton Sioux and Northern Cheyenne to fight back. This would become the longest war ever fought by the US Army, lasting over 40 of the 300 years of conflict with the Natives Nations, killing over 20,000 on either side, the balanced numbers eloquent testimony to the indomitable fighting spirit of the hugely under-armed and under-manned Native warriors. It would cost the US $150,000 a day – a peaceful and honest settlement would have cost a fraction of that. The massacre outraged Americans and Chivington, a Methodist lay preacher on a self-proclaimed mission to annihilate the Natives, was eventually dismissed after Colonel Edward Wynkoop's inquiry confirmed his guilt.

Despite Sand Creek, amazingly, Chief Black Kettle kept his faith in peace and sought protection at Fort Larned for his 400 surviving old men, women, and children. Inevitably, this eroded his following among the warriors even further, some, especially the fierce Cheyenne Dog Soldier society, who believed he had sold out to the whites, going to the extent of making death threats against him. Never in his life did Black Kettle harm any white person. The sympathetic Colonel Edward Wynkoop, who had earlier founded the city of Denver, settled them on the Washita River, giving Black Kettle another huge US flag with the assurance, "You will be totally safe under this flag. No soldier will ever attack it." The Chief proudly flew it on a tall pole beside his own tepee along with another large white flag. He continued to stay in camp there, still believing in the power of his flag despite many, including his wife, anxiously urging him to flee.

At daybreak on 27th November 1868, the vainglorious "boy general" of the Civil War, the 28-year-old Lieutenant Colonel George Armstrong Custer and his 7th Cavalry surrounded and attacked the village, sleeping peacefully under its twin flags, raining down death on the defenseless, to the accompaniment of a flamboyant "Garry Owen". After the mindless butchery of the innocents, Custer never hesitated to embroider the truth in his own interests, reported 103 warriors dead. A modern account by the US Centre of Military

History puts the number of dead at 50, almost all old men, women and children including Black Kettle and his wife. In reality, almost everyone in Black Kettle's village died. The warlike Cheyenne Dog Soldiers encamped nearby heard the firing and charged across to attack. It was too late. Fearing for his life, Custer rapidly retreated, not pausing till he was all the way back at Fort Supply, abandoning Major Thomas Elliott and his entire company to be cut off and killed. For Custer, this was his first "Indian battle"; his second, at the Little Bighorn, would be his last, where he would face real warriors in battle for the first time. Even at the Washita, had Black Kettle been a little closer to the big Cheyenne and Arapaho camp, Custer would probably not have lived to see the Little Bighorn. As a final touch of infamy, General Sheridan had their entire pony and mule herd slaughtered, over eight hundred animals.

"It's great that more and more people are visiting, and learning the truth," the Ranger tells me, "instead of General Sheridan's careful campaign of untruths and fabrications."

Controversy rages to this day over the official description of this event as a "battle". A sheepish Ranger explained to me that only 'battlefields' can be designated a National Park and hence.... a curious rationale for distorting history. I noticed that even Google Maps refers to it as a battlefield. It horrified all Native Nations and Colonel Wynkoop too. The latter immediately resigned in furious outrage while, for the Natives, this would inflame passions beyond quenching. Custer himself considered it normal military action. Americans, however, were incensed at the barbarity of the attack, yet again, after the earlier Sand Creek horror. Incredibly, some Custer apologists, even today, claim it may have been totally one-sided, but that it was not a massacre.

We must give credit where it is due. One of the great aspects of modern America is its honesty about its past, despite the prism of a multi-racial society. Rarely is there ever an attempt to ignore or whitewash unpalatable events or facts, but to tell it "warts and all". The Rangers here unambiguously naming it a massacre reflects that. I know of no other nation that is, by and large, as open and honest about the less salubrious portions of its ancestry.

It would be this blind self-assurance, born of his "victory" here on the Washita, that would be Custer's undoing at the Little Bighorn where he implicitly believed he could use the same tactics on a huge warrior village, led by the redoubtable Chiefs, Crazy Horse, and Sitting Bull. He would not live to regret his error. Today, all that remains of Black Kettle is a fading marker in an empty field, splotched with patches of brown grass, like old, dried blood.

Just 55 miles due east of this terrible field is a town that still, shockingly, commemorates its author, Custer City, just as, 10 miles south of gruesome Sand Creek sits a city commemorating the shameful Chivington. It seems inconceivable that such names survive unchanged. Walking the rough trail to the then riverside (the river has changed course in the 150 years since) to the massacre site, I pause in silent, somber contemplation of the inhumanity of man to man. I pray that Black Kettle and all the dead, on both sides, are finally at peace, with the grandfathers.

Like the pitiful survivors of the Washita, I drift in low spirits down that same road of ghosts, towards the same destination as theirs, Custer's Fort Supply. Driving along, as the sun got hotter and the glare harsher, I found I had left my two bottles of water behind in the motel refrigerator. Ah, well...

You have to love the wide, open roads of America! A dead-straight, smooth ribbon of concrete runs flat and unbroken through the heart of Kansas, all the way to the horizon and beyond. Open green fields on all sides rest easy on the eye, while the excellent sign-posting along the freeways makes it easy to navigate. I can finally understand the Americans' love of the road. I have not seen a single human in over 50 miles, and just the odd semi-trailer or two once in a long, long while. As the traffic fades to near extinction, my speedometer seems to imperceptibly inch higher of its own accord. The increase in velocity is so gradual that it is with a start I realize, at some point, I am hurtling down the 65-mph road at well over 120 mph! It would be well after my trip was over that I would discover the sobering fact that exceeding the speed limit beyond a certain point can earn you jail time, besides a fine! Whew! I sure dodged a bullet there.

Ever since I had begun my trip, my dear Garmin had been mysteriously chiming every so often. It was rather annoying but, try as I might, I could not figure out the reason. Now, with nothing else to do on these endless, mindless roads, I pondered this mystery afresh – and suddenly, had an epiphany! Of course! Every time I exceeded a posted speed limit, my faithful Garmin chimed, giving me fair warning. And, judging by the frequency of its chimes over the last week or so, I must have been a bit naughty! Sometimes, though, my friend Garmin made some rather strange observations - for instance, on a long, straight road, it suddenly warned of "Curves ahead." It could not have been referring to the road!

Town/village after town/village flashed by as I drove on. Passing three closed-down gas stations in three tiny, people-less hamlets, over 100 miles, I eyed my rapidly wilting fuel gauge with mounting concern. Fortunately, a live one finally hove into view, just as the gas indicator was contemplating its last fatal plunge to "Empty." By now, I too was beginning to feel hungry but had not spotted a single café, or even a general store in the pastoral settlements I passed. Eventually, I had to save myself from starvation with my trusty Lyallpur Navrattan Mixture. It was then that I realized, when folks talk of the vast, empty heartland of America, they really do mean empty! The occasional intriguing road sign, or place name, broke the sheer monotony of the endless, vacant fields, such as "Dead Warrior Creek," which I passed now, and "Dead Horse Creek" which would flash by a little later. The Great Plains commemorate death a lot.

More than an hour later, I turned off the imaginatively named Road 1900 towards Fort Supply. Driving blithely towards the gates of what I assumed to be the historic Fort, an aggressive security cruiser charged out of somewhere and angrily flagged me to a stop. Only then did it register on me that the high-security fencing all around the site was not consistent with an abandoned, historic ruin! Fort Supply has become a psychiatric asylum and correctional facility, and security shooed me away with impatient annoyance. Since the historic part of Fort Supply opened only on request, I had made an appointment with its Curator, Taylor Hunter, to access it. However, Taylor's name cut no ice with the officers and they told me, in no uncertain terms, to go back to the main road and wait for him there. Today was not my day for pleasantries with the police. I did not have to wait long on the shoulder of the lonely road before Taylor turned up and led me to the four gutted buildings that are all that remains of the once huge fort. The cop car had not moved from its vigil all this while, keeping a doleful vulture's eye on me, and even now, followed me all the way to the historic area to ensure I did no evil. Only after Taylor and I had parked at the site did they reluctantly drive away. I heaved a sigh of relief.

Taylor showed me around with enthusiasm, and it was clear he is passionate about his charge. He is a local and has been looking after the fairly badly neglected backwater site for years. Finding a rare, genuinely interested audience in me, he waxed eloquent about the history of the place. Sadly, he did not have very much material to work with as little worthwhile remains today. Even in its heyday, it was just what its name implied, nothing more than a supply depot for Sheridan and Custer. I had stopped by only to commune with the ghosts of the Cheyenne survivors of the Washita who were brought here. It did not take long, as even their ghosts seem to have abandoned the place. Fort Supply remains today, as it was then, just a dusty little footnote to history.

I was now well into the Kansas heartland. Always rich and fertile, in the 1930s over-cultivation and over-grazing by cattle ranchers, followed by a crippling drought, killed off all the prairie grass that protected the soil, turning Kansas into a giant dustbowl for barren decades to come. Slowly, with modern agrarian practices being introduced, the land has been coaxed back to health and it now, once again, delivers huge crops of wheat, corn, soybeans, and many other staples besides hosting the ubiquitous herds of beef cattle. The Canadian River crossed my path repeatedly. From the land of the Cherokee, Apache, and Comanche, I was now in the land of the Southern Cheyenne.

As I continued to ride the I-40, I felt a decided rocking motion. I was initially at a bit of a loss to account for this, till I realized that powerful winds off the high plains were giving my little Ford's suspension a workout. I remembered then, this is Kansas, where winds are the strongest on the entire Continent and tornadoes frequent. Ah, tornadoes – I scanned the horizon anxiously.

Two hours later, I finally rolled into legendary Dodge City. It had been quite a detour to visit Dodge, and I wondered if it would be worth the hours of extra driving.

While the late afternoon sun slowly melted into the horizon, I looked for a laundry as my clothes, by this time, most definitely needed refreshing. My fragrant presence easily outdid the beef milling around. I eventually tracked down what, I suspect, is the sole laundry in Dodge City, only to find it closed for Memorial Day. I had not even realized it was a major American holiday today. Further searching finally unearthed a coin laundry at my Motel. In the end, it worked out well – except that I could not figure out where, or how, to get the detergent for it. So, it ended up being just a wash in hot water, but it did the trick. I think!

Clockwise from top left: Quirky Boot Hill gravestones, Dodge City; Boot Hill, Dodge City.

Clockwise from top All that remains today of famed Fort Laramie; telegram from Fort Robinson informing the President of the death of Crazy Horse; the ill-fated Adjutant's Office where Crazy Horse died; Army marker of the Grattan fight (note the wording).

DAY 8: 28 MAY - GET THE HECK OUT OF DODGE!

Last evening, I rode wearily into town, though, unlike the star of TV's "Gunsmoke" or Wyatt Earp, Doc Holliday and their ilk, I rode in on four wheels. Still, it had been a long, hard 550-kilometer ride, through the utterly somniferous, rural heartland of Kansas, roughly following the old Chisholm Trail on which ten million Texas Longhorn cattle moved to the Dodge City railhead, in another age. Engrossing road signs broke the monotony, with not a single human or animal to be seen for more than fifty miles at a stretch. In Dodge, I met "Butter & Egg Road". Residents here fought to prevent its name being changed to "Lariat." I kid you not! I crossed the Arkansas

River, informally marking the divide between the southern and northern Great Plains; traveled from Oklahoma into Kansas; from the radio exhorting you to "Rahse to the Oklahoma kahnd of lahfe" to, well, not much else, as I had yet to find anything other than cattle living in Kansas! Over the coming days, the FM would offer me a scintillating selection of Christian ministry or cattle auction prices...and absolutely nothing else.

Looking out over the fields, home to the world's richest wheat and cattle industries, it is difficult to visualize that it was the great, devastated dustbowl of America in the 1930s. I had traveled this long road for a glimpse of the other side of the Frontier experience – the rowdy, bawdy, gutsy, no-holds-barred world of enterprising settlers, cowboys, miners, trappers, railroad men, Chinamen. While Dodge City was not a direct result of the clash of civilizations, it was a landmark of that era – much like another I visited some years ago, Tombstone, Arizona. These remarkable pioneers built the America we know. In 1872, a bar – what else! – set up in a tent on the Santa Fe Trail birthed Dodge. Variously nicknamed "Wicked, little city", "Sodom of the West" and more politely, "Queen of the Cow Towns", Dodge City achieved international fame with Marshall Dillon's unforgettable threat that has become part of the lexicon. Today, it welcomes tourists with "Get the heck INTO Dodge!" and has even renamed a major street, Gunsmoke.

Dodge really came into its own, though, with the arrival of the Santa Fe Railroad, starting its cow-town era. Even today, beef accounts for over 60% of its economy.

Dodge was the end of the very long trail for cowboys, often riding over 1500 miles, desperate to blow their earnings on alcohol, women, clothes, – and a bath. The railroad eventually replaced the old cowboy herding trails, but it still claims to be "The Cowboy Capital of the World". It was the originator of such homespun Vaquero wisdom as "Fear the goat from the front, the mule from the back, and man from all sides." However, it earned its place in folklore primarily through its colorful lawmen – Wyatt, Morgan & Virgil Earp, Bat Masterson, and their friend, the gunslinger dentist,

Doc Holliday. The foursome, Earps and Holliday, would later move to Tombstone, where they shot down the notorious Clancy Gang, immortalized in Hollywood's "Gunfight at the OK Corral". Little known of Wyatt Earp, the archetypal lawman, his career included arrests for horse thieving, gambling, escaping jail, and being fined for "keeping and being found in a house of ill-fame"!

Drifting along Front Street, I marvel at the effort made to recreate the atmosphere of its heyday, despite so few artifacts surviving. The original Santa Fe Railroad Station is now home to The Depot Theatre. A curiosity, in this most curious town, is that the Kansas Teachers Hall of Fame hosts the Gunfighters Waxwork Museum. I had wanted to visit this first-of-its-kind Hall of Fame dedicated to teachers, as a salute to my teacher-wife. However, on hauling myself up the hill to the little house, I discovered Memorial Day had struck again! Both exhibits were closed for the entire holiday weekend and I had to walk away, just saluting it from the road. The best-laid plans of mice and men...

Despite the boiling day, a strong breeze made it pleasant enough to wander around town. The place is dominated by Cargill Corporation's mammoth meat processing plants, which are rather less than scenic. Taking in the few hundred meters of the single street of interest, I realized it is more a small town than a real city. I should have planned to spend just one day in Dodge City instead of two. There is not much for the second day. Most places being closed for Memorial Day ensured it an even more somnolent atmosphere. So, I visited everything except its piece de resistance, Boot Hill, which I would hold back for tomorrow, like a child hoarding a lollipop.

First off, I took the Trolley Tour from the Visitor Centre to get an overview of the place – and to discover if there really is life beyond Front Street. I was feeling like I had landed in Potemkin's Village. The picturesque red 'trolley' trundled off to a hearty (recorded) Kansas welcome. As it threaded its way through the streets of Dodge, the commentary was interesting and, contrary to my preconceived notions, non-racist! However, it was obvious that it voiced the worldview of those who believe God created the land to be cultivated and not "wasted" chasing buffalo on. Despite the lack of any real animosity towards them, there is little understanding of Native Americans here, even today. At nearby Fort Dodge, is a nauseating glorification of Custer, with no effort to critically examine his often shameful legacy. The Native Americans have been consigned to the doldrums of history. It reminded me of John Wilson's insightful comment, "...a history that despite (or perhaps because of) the millions of words devoted to it remains oddly suppressed and hidden...a complex, elusive and hugely misunderstood history."

Unlike Army soldiers, who were mercenaries fighting for a wage, Native warriors were born to be warriors and trained intensively from a very early age. Hardly surprisingly, the Army found itself losing to the superior warcraft of the Natives who fought much as they hunted, relying more on tactics than technology. It was the Native American warrior who first introduced the European to guerrilla warfare. Facing constant defeats, General Sheridan unleashed the utterly heartless scorched earth, or Total War, a concept he had perfected in the Shenandoah Valley during the Civil War. The teeming multitudes of buffalo on the Great Plains were the 'general store' of the Natives, providing them with everything they needed for survival, from food to shelter, weapons, clothing, toys, and tools. With the arrival of the Kansas Pacific Railroad, Sheridan encouraged hordes of buffalo hunters to descend upon the Plains, in blatant violation of treaties expressly forbidding them to hunt buffalo south of the Arkansas River, and kill the animals indiscriminately. Buffalo skins were in great demand on the Eastern seaboard, but massive mountains of surplus meat were simply left to putrefy in the sun, all across the Plains. This sacrilegious waste of a God-given resource shocked the Natives perhaps more than any other action of the wasicu. In very short order, this policy resulted in the bison being driven to the very edge of extinction, and the Native nations starved onto Reservations, at the uncertain mercy of the white man's annuities.

As Chief Spotted Eagle expressed it, "The driving off of the Buffalo was death to my race and we would rather have fought, even knowing we would be beaten in the end."

The majestic buffalo gradually morphed into placid Longhorn beef on the Great Plains. An entire way of life silently faded to black.

In 1877 Dodge had just 1000 residents (13 of whom they recorded as being 'religious people') but as many as 16 saloons, including the most famous one of them all, the Long Branch Saloon. Indeed, a saloonkeeper, George Hinkle, eventually defeated the legendary Bat Masterson in an election for Sheriff. As the trolley rolled out of town into the surrounding countryside, I had my first glimpse of sprawling beef feedlots, each with 45,000 or more heads of cattle. For a fleeting moment, the pungent smell of lowing herds milling about wafted nostalgia for the cattle driving days of times gone by.

An apocryphal joke illustrates attitudes to the Dodge of old. A grizzled old prospector boarded a train somewhere in Kansas. When the conductor asked the old-timer for his destination, he growled, "Hell". The weary conductor replied, "That will be 65 cents, and get off at Dodge."

Across from the old Santa Fe Depot stands the statue of Wyatt Earp, the legendary lawman credited with finally taming "the toughest town on the map." Near him is a marker for the 100th Meridian which was the border for the Louisiana Purchase. However, nowhere in Dodge did I find any mention of the largely unknown fact that it also sits on the world's largest underground aquifer.

Near the Visitor Centre, I was fascinated to find one of the old giant steam locomotives of the Kansas Pacific Railroad on display. Disappointingly, access to the cab was chained off to the public, though I could not imagine why. It is unlikely anyone could steal that monster for a joyride. I carefully averted my eyes from Boot Hill, just behind it, still much like a child hoarding a treat for later!

DAY 9: 29 MAY - TORNADO ON MY TAIL

The night sky, last evening, was heaving with overcast, full of lightning. I desperately want to write "The sky was full of portents," but just cannot think of anything it might have portended! Strangely, I heard very little thunder. The clouds threatened an imminent deluge. To add to the atmospherics, they broadcast multiple tornado warnings on radio, TV, and text messages to my mobile. I was just beginning to worry a little, hoping the weather would not disrupt my trip, but the Motel Receptionist assured me "most tornadoes dodge Dodge." Eventually, the weather only flattered to deceive.

I was no longer surprised to find that the owner of this Motel, too, is a Gujarati from Surat in India. The room was large and well furnished, though breakfast, again, must have left its American guests, whose appetites are a tad better than mine, feeling they had suffered scorched earth tactics. My phone still refused to pick up any GSM signal. Contacting the T-Mobile helpdesk online elicited little elucidation. I worried my phone itself might be kaput.

As the day wore on, I finally treated myself to the outstanding, experiential Boot Hill Museum. Built on the old Boot Hill Cemetery, it houses fascinating relics of the Old West and, it is said, not a few famous ghosts, besides a painstaking recreation of the original Front Street, with live shops served by staff in period costume and personality. The John Tyler Tonsorial Parlor, for instance, offered a shave, haircut, bath – and dentistry, with sometimes comic consequences. Dodge City's first newspaper, "The Front Street Times" has its print shop here. During the slow summer months, it printed "Reward" posters for wanted outlaws. The Undertaker's shop has a prominent place, as is only to be expected in a town of gunslingers. Of the 25 establishments on Front Street, no less than 7 are saloons! The general store, bar and restaurant are 'live' establishments, open for business. The Boot Hill Cemetery, where quite a few characters were "planted," possesses a collection of enthralling headstones. The first was for Black Jack who "died with his boots on", giving Boot Hill its name. Henry Callahan was hanged as a horse thief – though, apparently, he was not really! Sharpshooter Steve O'Hara was killed in a duel when "red-eye ruined his deadeye." The only 'lady' planted here is Lizzie Palmer, a "soiled dove" killed in a barroom brawl with another over the affections of Bat Masterson, whose gun is proudly displayed on Front Street. Atop the hill, tiny Fort Dodge Jail, from 1865, has the look of a modern port-a-loo. Hours later, I head to the attraction that is universally popular with children and adults alike, the shoot-out on Front Street, dramatically scheduled at high noon and dusk.

After a vigorous exchange of gunfire, with much smoke, noise, and hollerin' without undue concern for realism, the resurrected gunslingers turn bartenders for the period Long Branch Variety Show. The old centerpiece of "Gunsmoke", and the nearby China Doll brothel, had defined the Dodge of old. True to its roots, in 2009 Boot Hill became the first State-owned casino in America.

I followed the torrent of tourists into the dining room for another authentic "country-style" dinner. I soon realized that I was, as usual, the only Injun in a roomful of cowboys. By now I was certain I was the only non-white person in the entire State of Kansas. However, contrary to what popular myth and legend had me expecting, I was treated exactly as a roomful of Injuns would have treated the Lone Ranger – with friendly, benevolent indifference. My second experience of chuck-wagon food had me commiserating with those old settlers. It is, basically, a low-cost meal with, these days, a high price-tag. Those settlers would surely have killed for a good curry!

While its variety may have left a mite to be desired, the quantity was no problem at all, as generous helpings were freely doled out. The servers were extra cordial to me, an obvious foreigner. While I struggled to finish even half my first helping, the servers loudly announced, "We have seconds and thirds, so don't feel shy."

I watched in awe as most customers showed just how un-shy they were in such matters! Strangely, in a land of chronic obesity, I found it difficult to find sugar-free desserts anywhere.

Feeding time at the trough over, we headed to the Bar to watch the vaunted Long Branch Variety Show. Presented with great humor and vigor, it was a blend of jokes, songs, and stage can-can dance, evocative of a bygone era. I have to doff my figurative hat to the enthusiasm and verve all the actors brought to the show. It was a great way to end the evening.

As I headed back to the Rodeway Inn, the heavy black clouds finally burst, unleashing torrents of rain and lightning. Tornado warning sirens shrieked continually; urgent "severe thunderstorm" notifications kept flashing up on TV; the black, louring overcast obliterated the evening sky. The Weather Channel showed a live feed of heavy clouds beginning to swirl into an angry tornado on the nearby Oklahoma border that I crossed two days ago.

Finally, as the crowning piece of drama, the Motel Receptionist called to warn me, "Chandra, please be ready to take shelter in your bathtub. Take all your things with you, and all the sheets off your bed."

Bathtub? Bedsheets? The message was alarming, but somehow her rather laconic delivery made me suspect it was a routine warning that did not really need to be heeded. Could it be that much worse than the monsoon back in India? I snuggled contrarily in my bed, enjoying the celestial pyrotechnics. I figured, even if tornadoes do dodge Dodge, I would be happy to get the heck out of tornado country. Some Dodge City farewell, that!

Tomorrow, as I head the heck out of "the wickedest little town in America", I shall look back with affection at this living relic of a boisterous century where folks lived hard, worked hard, conned hard and died hard. Apparently, they even tornado hard!

DAY 10: 30 MAY - NABBED!

Heading out of Dodge City, the morning fog soon burned away into a bright, hot day. A large sign marks the spot where the original Santa Fe Trail ruts are still allegedly visible. All I found was tall, thick prairie grass as far as the eye could see, undoubtedly concealing the usual mass of beady-eyed rattlesnakes, eyeing me with dripping fangs. Disappointed, I carried on, and disappointed they probably went back to biting others.

The arrow-straight road was smooth and empty for hundreds of miles. Almost two hours out, past Cimarron and Dighton on KS-23, I had become complacent. Unnoticed, my speedometer again crept up towards 120 mph on the 65 mph road. I zoomed through the tiny town (more a village, really) of Gove, Kansas and, chuckling to myself at its quaintness, used my dashcam to video the entire two minutes it took to traverse it. I smiled at the cute little Courthouse. Just imagine! A tiny village with its own tiny Courthouse! Before I knew it, I had blown out of town, back into the countryside.

I began chasing a long-chassis truck to get past. It seemed to take longer than I expected and I was becoming frustrated at his not allowing me through. He seemed to keep flashing his hazards at me, for some annoying reason. Fuming, I glanced up at my mirror and, to my horror, realized that a police cruiser was chasing me down with all his rooftop Christmas-tree lights flashing angrily. It finally dawned on me that the truck ahead had been trying to warn me about the trooper. As I slowed to the roadside, I was excited, "Just like the movies!"

Then, I remembered that in those same movies, the cops were almost always bad dudes, especially when dealing with colored guys! Nervously, I kept both hands conspicuously in sight on the steering wheel, as those movies had taught me to.

The officer walked up, "Sir, I had you clocked at 91, in a 65 zone."

My supposedly shocked, "Really, Officer? 91?" didn't cut it, even with me.

With the patience born of hearing the same excuses every day, he replied, "Yes sir, you were trucking right along. Your License and Rental Agreement, please."

He was pleasant, courteous, and almost apologetic, "Sir, if it was on the Interstate, I could probably have given it a pass, but on little KS-23...," he just shook his head in disbelief.

I made sure he understood the Rental Agreement was in the glove box as I reached veeeeery slowly to open it. He must have realized I watched too many cop movies.

On seeing my Oman driving license, he asked when I was leaving the country. I said, "In a month."

He mulled the situation for a while, knowing I would be long gone by the time their mailed Citation reached me and there was nothing he could do about it.

Turning to me, he asked, "Sir, would you be willing to come back with me to the County Courthouse and pay your fine? It's only 10 miles back, and I will reduce your fine a little if you cooperate."

As he had been gentlemanly about the unfortunate necessity of fining me, and had not even shot me, and since I was in the wrong anyway, I agreed with a faux-pious mea culpa expression. To my chagrin, it was to the dinky little Courthouse in Gove, about which I had laughed into my video just a short while ago, that I followed the Police cruiser, like a leashed dog. The Court Clerk who collected my fine was friendly and, again, almost apologetic. Neither treated me like I was the one in the dock. Thankful to be free and un-shot, though $221.52 the poorer (discounted – just like Oman! – from

$280), I continued on my way, considerably chastened and law-abiding once more. Kansas cops, Hollywood does you no favors!

To Dodge, and then today, have been the two longest drives of the trip – over 1100 kilometers with an overnight at a charming little hamlet called Lewellen. This was about the halfway point of my odyssey. It was also where I changed time zones to Mountain Time. It had been a tiring day through the flat and unexciting country. It must have been great for horses and buffalo in them days. The gentle, rhythmic rocking of the car over the joints in the concrete road felt not unlike riding a horse. As the monotony almost lulled me to sleep, I hastily slapped myself awake and switched on some loud classical music – oh, blissful improvement on cattle and Christ! – now coming out of nearby Nebraska. I passed a rural signpost pointing, utterly incongruously, to "Achilles".

Only on crossing my second State line, into Nebraska, near McCook, did the flat land finally develop gentle contours, the road take on curves, little lakes zip by and the greenery seem a richer emerald. But still nary a soul anywhere. Now, there were not even the cattle that populated Kansas. And when I say totally devoid of life, I really do mean totally! Nebraska, a prettier Kansas, has more acreage with no life than I have seen anywhere else – it gives you an idea of just how massive this country is, what "Big Sky" means. What an awesome achievement to bring those millions of acres under human tillage.

Near Ogllalla, I finally reached the history-soaked North Platte River. I had arrived in the land of the Lakota. Canta waste upo, a warm-hearted welcome!

Back on the road, after stopping briefly to gaze at the North Platte River, I mused on the confusion of numbers on so many US roads. Often, the same stretch of freeway has several numeric designators and sometimes, to thoroughly confound the confusion, with a suffix of "Byp" (Bypass) or "Alt" (Alternate) or, most puzzling of all, "Bus" (Business) tacked on. If there is a method in this madness, for the life of me, I could not figure it out. Some mysteries are just meant to remain mysterious.

Lewellen Lodge is a very pleasant Bed & Breakfast tucked away in a quiet little corner of this sleepy transit village. The rooms are generous suites with a bedroom attached to a sitting room. Though its air-conditioning is slightly lethargic, the rustic sunset framing my window was exquisitely tranquil and picturesque. I wondered if the village's founders were Welsh. However, the siren call of my bed won out over curiosity. As I lay abed that night, I heard voices, coughing and snoring through my bedroom wall from the adjoining room. The lonely, midnight whistle of a passing freight train finally lulled me to sleep.

The next morning, I discovered that my room is the last one in that wing; there was nothing beyond my bedroom wall!

DAY 11: 31 MAY - TREACHERY

Almost three hours down the road, all tiredness vanished as I approached fabled Fort Laramie, the scene of so much that was good and bad on the Frontier. Somewhere, I had crossed another State line into Wyoming. I turned off the black anaconda that is US-26 and coiled my way past the placidly flowing North Platte River, a silent witness to centuries. There ahead, on the promontory of its namesake river, awaited Fort Laramie, the setting of so many momentous treaties and treacheries, now just silent, crumbling ruins. One of the few surviving structures, Old Bedlam, the bachelor officers' quarters built in 1849, is the oldest surviving building in the state of Wyoming. Founded by 'Mountain Man' William Sublette, the Army took it over, and hosted the infamous Treaty of 1868 guaranteeing the Lakota their sacred Black Hills would remain theirs forever, "as long as the grass shall grow and the waters flow".

As in most US Treaties, it expounded that "the Government of the United States desires peace and pledges its honor to uphold it." Shortly thereafter, the 'discovery' of gold in the Black Hills by an illegal expedition escorted by Custer, posturing as the savior of the recession-facing national economy, and hoping thereby to catapult himself into the Presidency, easily trumped honor. The grass, as I saw, was still growing and the water flowing. But the Black Hills no longer belong to the Lakota, despite that sovereign promise.

An earlier Laramie Treaty signed at the nearby confluence of Horse Creek and the Platte River, slightly east of the present Wyoming-Nebraska State line, did ensure peace for three years. I paused at the marker to gaze out over the momentous site, now on private farmland. I wondered if the farmer realizes he is tilling a piece of Western history. That peace lasted till yet another inexperienced, arrogant young Lieutenant, John Grattan, instigated an unnecessary fight east of here on the Oregon Trail, almost within sight of the Fort as the crow flies. That unleashed a generation of bloody war onto the Great Plains, setting the Continent inexorably on the gore-soaked path that would eventually lead to Wounded Knee. The Lakota had only wanted to ensure their freedom to follow and hunt the buffalo, their 'general store' from which they derived everything they needed. Unscrupulous settlers eventually stole even that, wantonly destroying about 60 million buffalo in a stunningly savage "scorched earth" tactic to defeat the warriors the Army could not in war.

The true tragedy of entirely avoidable bloodshed and genocide on the Great Plains is, to a very large extent, the tragedy of Army command reposed in the hands of inexperienced, arrogant leaders unfit to command. Even at its highest levels, Generals who were unabashedly racist and genocidal commanded the Army. Ethics never entered the equation. It was in the same tradition as the Puritans' destruction of the Pequots at Mystic, which created a precedent for later genocidal wars. Similar in spirit to the English who murdered 200 Chiskiacks just after signing a treaty with them, by having them toast their "eternal friendship" with poisoned sack.

And this despite the fact that fully half the Iroquois perished in the War of Independence, fighting for the Crown.

A starving, lame old cow had strayed from the Mormons' wagon-train into the Lakota camp and been killed by a Minneconjou visitor. Grattan was instructed to arrest the offender. The brash Lieutenant, the arrogance of inexperience fuelling his lust for glory, egged on by the avaricious settlers, refused to understand the Lakota code of hospitality absolutely forbade the giving up of a guest under their roof. He tried to force the issue, despite being offered more than generous compensation for the old cow. The resultant battle (despite being instigated by Grattan, even today referred to as a 'massacre' on the Army site marker that I eventually located, down a narrow, rutted country road, now on private farmland) culminated in the death of all 30 soldiers and the respected Brule Chief, Conquering Bear. Ironically, he had been appointed overall Chief of all the Lakota by the wasicu Fort commander himself, despite such a position being completely alien to the Lakota themselves. This battle would set fire to the Great Plains and lead directly to the longest war ever fought by the United States.

This tragedy was exacerbated, soon after, by General William Harney killing over a hundred innocent Lakota at Blue Water Creek, the infamous act earning him the derogatory nickname of "Squaw Killer" from his own people. A youthful Crazy Horse possibly witnessed the massacre and would never forget it, becoming the Army's most implacable foe in the years ahead – a foe it never defeated. Partly because of this remarkable antagonist, between 1865 and 1890 the Frontier Army suffered a stunning 33% desertion, according to the National Parks Service brochure.

Several treaties were signed at Fort Laramie, besides the controversial Treaty of 1868, but not a single one was ever honored by the Government. A modern Princeton University study found that the Government signed, and dishonored, over 600 treaties with the Natives. The Natives, for their part, did not willfully violate a single one. Honour, clearly, had a different meaning for each side. Over the coming years, many celebrated Civil War leaders, such as

Generals Sherman, Sheridan and Miles, and the infamous Colonels, Custer and Kit Carson, would indelibly stain their escutcheons with unrelenting brutality and savagery towards the, mainly non-combatant, Native populations. Sheridan made no distinction between hostile and friendly Natives and is on record as saying, "I am of the belief that these Indians require to be soundly whipped, and the ringleaders in the present trouble hung, their ponies killed and such destruction of their property as will make them very poor."

Decades earlier, during Pontiac's War, Baron Jeffery Amherst, later to be made a Field Marshall, even initiated primitive germ warfare, cynically ordering, "...send the smallpox among all disaffected tribes."

The few insightful and visionary officers, such as General George Crook and Colonel Edward Wynkoop, were labeled 'Indian lovers' and found their military careers withered on the vine.

The Fort of so many ghosts was finally decommissioned and sold off in 1890.

Unlike the bluntly honest one at the Washita, the Laramie Ranger video is more, I suppose, politically correct. The guns have long fallen silent; the smoke of many peace pipes dispersed to the four directions. Great warriors do not tread the earth anymore and treachery is no longer rife here. Not much remains to tell its extraordinary tale but what little does, bears mute testimony to the weighty hand of history.

Leaving Fort Laramie, I headed back into Nebraska en route to South Dakota. The terrain had become distinctly hillier, more picturesque, and the temperature dropped appreciably. To add to my collection of strange place and road names, I passed "Cook Oil Road," noticing "Shady Rest Motel" on the way. Fortunately, that was not my destination. A large billboard carried a corporate advertisement for "Wife Insurance." I never found out what that was all about.

I stopped briefly at the Fort Laramie–Fort Robinson Trail Marker, said to still show the ruts from General Sheridan's 1874 Sioux campaign. Unfortunately, like the Santa Fe Trail ruts, I saw no sign of them; the fields enveloped in thick, tall prairie grass. I consoled myself with a touch of historical imagination instead.

Heading down the Bridges and Buttes Highway, I drove into Fort Robinson, one of the key destinations on my Great Plains pilgrimage. Despite its abysmally uninformative and unhelpful website, I had eventually hunted down and reserved a room at the original Administration Building of the Fort, now converted into the Fort Robinson Lodge, one of the few surviving structures from that time, located right at the heart of the fort. The room itself, up three baggage-hauling flights of stairs without an elevator, was pleasant and spacious with a sweeping view of the surrounding area. There was no TV and, for the first time on my trip, I found the wi-fi signal very poor, having to keep wandering about the building to pick up or send messages. Since the sun was swooning into the horizon, I held off exploring the Fort itself for the next day and instead headed off in search of the nearby Red Cloud Agency. It was very poorly signposted, but that could not deter a determined aficionado of times past.

After a fair bit of, literally, beating about the bush, I eventually stumbled upon the lonely marker amid a tumultuous sea of chest-high prairie grass. I stood at the site, as always wary of the rattlesnakes that infest the area (does America have the largest rattlesnake population in the world? They seem to be everywhere!), and gazed across the meadow towards the wild buttes in the distance. Perhaps I thought, this is fitting. The Red Cloud Agency sleeps under a protective carpet of Nature, safely distant from the strife of the soldiers' Fort and the din of uncaring, and ignorant, holidaymakers.

DAY 12: 1 JUNE - MURDER MOST FOUL

Murder, treachery, betrayal, back-stabbing, and sheer infamy – tragic Fort Robinson experienced it all, in one epochal incident. For me, this is a pilgrimage, not tourism. Here, one of the greatest American heroes, the Strange Man of the Oglala Lakota, Tasunko Witko, Crazy Horse, was treacherously betrayed and murdered. The indomitable warrior, the protean enigma the entire US Army could never overcome, finally fell to a stab in the back. I sat on the grass for well over an hour, in moody reflection on his extraordinary life, contemplating this giant among men with reverence and awe, at the exact spot where a murderous bayonet ended it all, now marked by a simple quartz cairn. This is hallowed ground, almost a Native Golgotha.

By May 1877, when he finally rode into the Red Cloud Agency to lay down weapons, Crazy Horse's reputation was much larger than life. The soldiers', and their commanders', inordinate fear of him was clear in the fact that, to escort this single warrior into Fort Robinson, unarmed and without his warriors, they felt a contingent of over 400 heavily armed soldiers was necessary. It was a parade of the proud and unconquered, heads high, something that would inflame wild jealousy in the more easily surrendered old warhorses, Red Cloud and Spotted Tail. An enigma even to his own people, this loner was that rare, intellectual war leader able to clearly understand the battle tactics of his enemy, visualize the changes needed to his own and, most remarkably, inspire his followers to join battle on his terms. This was unheard of as both living and fighting, for the Lakota warrior, was always individual and private, taking orders from no one, following only those who earned his respect and loyalty through his deeds and life values, unlike the Europeans who were good at achieving collective goals as a coordinated team. "Today is a good day to die" was the Lakota creed. Hence, his triumphs were legendary, on a different level to those of even Red Cloud, Sitting Bull, Cochise, Geronimo, and that entire remarkable pantheon.

Renowned for his extraordinary personal courage, and utter fearlessness in battle, a classic individualist instinctively distrustful of group psychology, he honed his skills fighting the Lakota's traditional enemies, the Blackfeet, Crow, and Pawnee. Emerging victorious from the dust of those battles, he was honored as a war leader by his people, and even given the rarest of rare accolades, being made a bearer of the ancient, revered Lakota short lance, the highest possible Oglala war rank.

Alongside his renown in war, he was deeply respected for his charity and care for his people as well as for his deep humility and spirituality. Except for weapons, he kept no war spoils or insignia for himself, despite being entitled to do so by the code of the Kit Fox warrior society he belonged to, instead he always gave away everything, including valuable horses, to those of his people in need. Even in war, he stood out for the simple, unadorned modesty of his dress, in sharp contrast to the magnificent regalia common to war chiefs. Nor did he ever participate in the singing and dancing to celebrate victories, the narration of his achievements. He had little patience for the great pageants of Lakota ceremonial. His glories were sung only by others. This exceptional modesty and self-effacement were because of his nature but were reinforced by his powerful vision of the thunder beings. As Bray notes in his seminal work on Crazy Horse, even sitting with other Chiefs, this deeply humble man was at pains to show that he did not consider himself important.

Along the way, when he was not at war, Crazy Horse managed to have a tempestuous affair with a beautiful married squaw,

Black Buffalo Woman. In Lakota society, the woman has complete freedom of choice in the matter of a husband and may change one if she so chooses. However, her husband, No Water, a cousin of Red Cloud, took exception – rare in their milieu – and tried to shoot Crazy Horse. The great warrior recovered but, true to his magnanimous spirit, forgave No Water and returned Black Buffalo Woman, despite her wishes. She later gave birth to a light-haired, light-skinned son, though it was never established if he was Crazy Horse's. No Water, unusually small-spirited for a Lakota warrior, harbored an enduring hatred for Crazy Horse that would dog him to the end of his days.

Later, he married Black Shawl, who outlived him, passing away in 1927, though their only daughter succumbed to the white man's disease before she reached her youth. Crazy Horse, who doted on her and had named her They Are Afraid of Her, was away at the time, and on receiving the devastating news back in camp, went alone into known hostile territory, to locate her burial scaffold, and mourned there for three days with the little body clutched to his breast, oblivious to the great potential danger around him. The indomitable warrior was also very human; life would never be easy for him.

Back on the battlefield, he would defeat General George Crook in the valley of the Rosebud River, and then wipe out Custer and his entire unit at the Battle of the Little Bighorn. The Rosebud battle was especially noteworthy as he fought a force considerably larger than his own and infinitely better armed, but still sent them retreating all the way back to Fort Robinson, neutralizing Crook's crucial role in Sheridan's pincer campaign against the Lakota.

After these glorious victories, though, primarily through the repeated exhortations of Red Cloud, he came to realize that the day of the Lakota warrior was in sunset. The buffalo were gone, Sitting Bull had moved to Canada, Red Cloud had become a wily, self-serving politician, warriors were dwindling while the supply of men and arms to the US Army was endless – the future was peace or perish. Political pressure mounted relentlessly on this most apolitical of men. The Lakota warrior was already riding into the dusty pages of history.

When Crazy Horse and his remaining people finally came into Fort Robinson, voluntarily, to lay down arms, eyewitnesses attested that Natives and soldiers alike lined both sides of the road, in awe. It was, one officer noted in astonishment, more a triumphal entry than surrender. This was the fabled warrior the US Army could not vanquish. He rode in proud, unconquered, accompanied by one of his closest, oldest and most trusted aides, Little Big Man, who had fought fiercely at his side in countless battles against the invaders and headed up his akicita, whose hatred of the wasicu was well known. It would be one of the greatest ironies of his life.

Ever a man of his word, a true Lakota warrior, for the next four months, he lived peacefully in the camp. However, despite being extremely modest and completely publicity averse, his renown and the respect shown him even by the Army, aroused the jealousy of Red Cloud and his step maternal Uncle, his childhood mentor and hero, Chief Spotted Tail. They manufactured false rumors, primarily by the insecure Red Cloud, deeply alarmed to see his own regard and following among his people dwindle every day. They spread tales to the credulous soldiers that Crazy Horse was plotting a return to the warpath. While no Native would have believed him capable of breaking his word, the fearful troops were easily persuaded. As they continued to inflame the soldiers' already extreme fear of him, additional troops were hastily drafted in. When they finally moved to arrest this single, unarmed man they felt the need for a force of not less than 400 soldiers and Native policemen.

Arriving at his camp, they discovered he had been forewarned and had ridden to his uncle, Spotted Tail's Reservation where he had every familial right to expect succor and shelter. To his eternal shame, his Uncle offered him a cold welcome. He was, instead, taken in by the loyal cousin from his birth mother's Minneconjou people, Touch the Clouds, the seven-foot giant chief who would be by his side to the bitter end. The well-intentioned Agent at this Reservation persuaded Crazy Horse to return to Fort Robinson, where he personally guaranteed his safety, a promise he should have known he could not honor.

As the sun descended towards the horizon on 5th September 1877, they rode back to Fort Robinson. Despite the assurances, Crazy Horse must have realized that he had arrived at a fateful crossroad. Curiously, weeks before coming in, he had had a vision of his death, which he carved into a boulder known as Owl Rock, at Deer Medicine Rock near Lame Deer, Montana. The picture depicts how he would be restrained by his own people while a soldier's bayonet inflicted two mortal wounds on his back. Though he realized he would not live long anywhere there were soldiers and Lakota together, he still brought his people in, to save them from starvation.

As it was late by the time they arrived, the Post Commander promised a meeting the next morning and ordered him to be given lodging. As they led him to it, Crazy Horse realized he was being taken into the Fort jail, to be imprisoned in irons. Instantly, he tried to escape, drawing a hidden knife, but he was immediately restrained from behind by one of the Native Scouts, allowing him to be mortally bayoneted in the back by an accompanying soldier, exactly as his vision had foretold. As the dying Crazy Horse turned to see who had restrained him, he looked into the eyes of Little Big Man, now wearing the coat of the hated wasicu. His own, trusted childhood friend and companion of many battles had betrayed his Chief, like a starving feral jackal yipping at the feet of a magnificent stag at bay. Exactly as Crazy Horse had foreseen during his arduous Vision Quest, so many long years ago, he died through the actions of his own people. With his last breath, a quiet greatness passed from the earth, never to return. The invincible warrior was 35 years old. With him, at the very end, were the ever-faithful Touch the Clouds, Crazy Horse's father, Worm, and the Post Doctor, his friend Dr. Valentin McGillycuddy, known to the Lakota as Tasunko Witko Kola, brother of Crazy Horse, or Wasicu Wakan, Holy White Man. It was the beginning of the long sadness.

Today, the Guardhouse outside which he was assassinated, and the Adjutant's Office where he was borne by the giant Touch the Clouds and breathed his last, are accurate replicas of the originals but tucked away in a remote corner. A scattering of quartz cairns on the grass in front of the office memorializes the exact site of the fatal stabbing, like splashes of blood. It is a fittingly simple memorial, for a humble magnificence.

The great soul of this simple, uneducated warrior frequently flashed with remarkable insights. On one such occasion, a hostile soldier taunted him, "Where are your lands now?"

His unruffled response was, "My lands are where my dead lie buried."

As it would be discovered later, even the generally sympathetic and principled General Crook was not immune to a touch of jealousy and resorted to the usual defense of the indefensible – following orders. He had enticed Crazy Horse to "come in" with the promise of his own Agency in his Powder River country, the last refuge of his way of life, to win this legendary warrior over to his command rather than that of his rival, General Nelson "Bear Coat" Miles, a promise that he had no authority to make and one he knew Washington would never honor. Once they got him onto the Red Cloud Agency, the overall theatre commander, General Sheridan, issued secret orders for him to either be assassinated or sent as a prisoner to Florida's deadly Dry Tortugas, a hellish little island lost in the ocean beyond Key West, from which no one ever returned, an American St. Helena. In this noxious effort, the very envious Red Cloud and Spotted Tail, who both imagined him a threat to their own supposed pre-eminence with the whites and were even keener than Sheridan to be rid of him permanently, ably abetted him. There is some indication that it was Red Cloud himself who egged Little Big Man on to restrain Crazy Horse, so the soldier could bayonet him. Over the Agency years, Red Cloud's stature had diminished massively in the eyes of both his warriors and the whites, who all saw the pitiful transformation of a once-great warrior into a petty, self-serving politician.

It is also telling that, in a society where familial bonds were so exceptionally powerful, while escaping to his Uncle's Rosebud Agency the day before his murder, Crazy Horse received no shelter or succor from him. No great surprise, then, that Spotted Tail, too, would in due course meet his end at the hands of one of his own people, within his own camp. Treachery breeds treachery. Crazy Horse's death was nothing short of State murder, and ultimately it lay squarely at the door of General George Crook who, on this critical occasion, failed his own values. Perhaps it was his sly revenge on the man who had so humiliatingly defeated him on the Rosebud and rubbed the noses of the US Cavalry in the dirt of the Powder River country for so long. As Bray eloquently put it, "the memory of magic and presence remains potent as example and inspiration."

Fort Robinson has been the site of many milestones. Founded in 1874, initially to guard the new Red Cloud Agency, it is where General Crook disbanded his troops after his defeat at the hands of Crazy Horse in the Rosebud River Valley. In 1878, the Cheyenne Chief Dull Knife's fleeing village was captured near here. He escaped from Fort Robinson the following year but was recaptured and killed. His brave but futile Cheyenne Outbreak is commemorated in their barrack but, again, from the Army's perspective. It became a railhead in 1886, and in 1890, troops from Fort Robinson took part in the horror at Wounded Knee. In modern times, it was used as a German POW camp in 1943 and finally closed as a military establishment in 1948. Today, it sits brooding uneasily between the past and the present.

What remains of Fort Robinson is disappointing. Only a few original structures survive, one of which is the barrack of the famed Buffalo Soldiers. African American soldiers were segregated in the US Army right up to World War II, and the story at Fort Robinson has largely been slanted to reflect age-old prejudices. The small Nebraska State Historical Society Museum, at the center of the site, narrates it unambiguously from the Army's perspective and tries to subtly whitewash its role, while diminishing the Crazy Horse/Red Cloud story. The far from balanced Museum video focuses more on dog training during World War II than the massive historic overhang of the Indian Wars. Even the actual site of Crazy Horse's murder, tucked away in one corner of the sprawling campus, is rarely referred to in the Fort's literature and is conspicuously absent from its maps. On inquiring about its location of the Museum's Curator, she gave me a vague, off-hand wave in the general direction I might find it, in a tone that clearly wondered why I would even bother.

Shortly after noon, I left Fort Robinson behind and headed for the Pine Ridge Reservation. It felt like moving out from under lowering storm clouds, back into the sunshine. Stopping briefly for a quick lunch at the forgettable little town of Chadron, I crossed my next State line, into South Dakota, making for Manderson-White Horse Creek for what, I was certain, would be a unique experience – spending two nights in a real Lakota tepee out on the open hillside. The last stretch of road was plain dirt, deeply rutted with passaging vehicles over the years. With no signposting at all, locating my Tepee-on-the-Prairie proved to be something of a labor of Hercules. Fortunately, contrary to what I had been led to expect, I found people on the Rez friendly and I drove up to several homes to ask directions. I would not have dared do that in many southern towns, for fear of being shot out of hand. Eventually, I located my AirBnB host's home.

Yes, this tepee must be among the more unusual offerings on AirBnB. It was not, strictly, a B&B, as there was a bed but no real breakfast on offer. My hostess was away but her in-laws received me graciously. They led me across a small field, up a gentle hill, and there, as its crowning glory, perched my promised tepee, in solitary splendor. The beautiful wooded hills surrounding the lush valley could not have been a more idyllic setting. As a final touch of perfection, a few wild mustangs pranced gracefully in the nearby meadow. Amidst this Eden, I remembered the serpent and asked my hosts about snakes.

With complete nonchalance, they responded, "Of course, there are plenty of snakes all around. Just don't bother them."

Bother *them*? I almost ran for an emergency change of underwear! In any case, he assured me, he had made a lot of noise recently, so they should stay away. With the 'door' of the tepee flapping open all night, I could only hope that no other wildlife would make a social call in the dark.

Only much later would I understand that this was not nonchalance at all on the part of my hosts, but something much more deeply rooted in their value system that advocates "mitakuye oyasin", we are all one. Native Americans believe innately that lack of respect for any growing or living thing soon leads to a lack of respect for human life itself. This Shinto-like reverence ensures they consider all living things "people". So, birds are "winged people," fish are "finned people," plants are "rooted people," animals are "four-legged people," even celestial bodies are "star people." Where most Westerners look on Nature as wild, savage or dangerous, in the Native perspective it is utterly beautiful and a limitless storehouse of knowledge and bounty. They prefer to sit or lie on the earth, to be in the closest possible contact with it, while Westerners distance themselves from it, on beds and chairs. The echoes of Shinto and the core of Celtic and Hindu faith are unmistakable. I recall seeing a Hindu swastika (not its reversed Nazi perversion) engraved on the ancient Anasazi walls of the Canyon de Chelley. The antique faiths have a strong underlying commonality.

After my hosts had spent a fair length of time hunting down a clean pillow and towel for me, I lay on my camp bed in the darkling, gazing out of the open flap of my tepee at that generous sprawl of stars overhead, like jewels scattered by a royal hand, listening to the symphony of crickets in the thickets, musing on another difference in the Natives' beliefs. They create everything in circles – tepees, camps, medicine wheels, even the "hoop of the people," as they believe Nature creates everything in circles. Contrasted with this, the colonizers created everything in squares and straight lines – houses, camps, parade grounds, machines. Curious.

Seemingly out of nowhere, I recalled the Powhatan Chief, Wahunsonacock's melancholy perplexity in 1609, "Why should you take by force that from us which you can have freely by love? Why should you destroy us, who have provided you with food?"

The same people from whose constitution Benjamin Franklin drew elements for planning the US confederation. Those whom James Wilson describes as "...bittersweet figments living on rather wispily in the annual Thanksgiving celebration and the litany of melodic Algonquin place names that still haunt the landscape."

Lulled by a cool breeze, I drifted gently off to sleep, untroubled by concerns of creepies crawling through my open tepee flap, marveling at the spectrum of human thought and understanding.

DAY 13: 2 JUNE - REQUIEM

I woke to another spirit-lifting Kodachrome day, a cold 10 Celsius. It was a surprisingly comfortable night and, opening my eyes to the stunning beauty of unspoiled Nature all around, heralded by birdsong everywhere, was pure ambrosia for the soul. It was 7 am and there was not a soul stirring anywhere.

Even my pen was reluctant to wake up as I sat down to make notes in my diary, in that crisp, clean cold. If this is mid-summer, I mused, I do not want to be here in winter! My Lakota tepee is tucked away in a remote nook of the Pine Ridge Reservation. Upon its slight, breezy rise, in lone magnificence, the only mod cons it had were a camp bed and sleeping bag. Getting up reluctantly, I went in search of the toilet; this turned out to be a bit of an adventure. To brush my teeth, I located a lonely outdoor basin with a bucket of water sitting beside it. Wastewater drained through a plastic pipe below, splashing onto the ground. Okaaaay...but now I needed to locate the place for my morning 'meditations'. This turned out to be on the other side of the wooden wall on which the basin hung, an outhouse without even the suggestion of a door. Communing with Nature took on a whole new meaning. I peered uncertainly in at this most non-urban contraption and realized it was just a deep hole in the ground, surmounted by a weary toilet seat. The pitch dark of the hole could easily conceal a small animal – or worse, a reptile just waiting to sink its fangs into my tender, unsuspecting rump. However, since Nature will not be denied, I had no choice but to mutter a prayer and perch unhappily.

A few of the feral mustangs ambled over and looked in on me through the open flap, evincing a friendly interest in the proceedings. The light, solar-electrified fence (showing it to me, last evening, my host's mother-in-law, Whiteface, had deadpanned, "Want to touch it?") was obviously beneath contempt for them. The strong breeze provided a blessed deodorizer as I perched apprehensively above what was, effectively, a rotting compost heap. Ruminating on life, I looked out over the landscape and noticed the 'shower'. This was an open-to-Nature wooden frame, with a big plastic drum balanced precariously on top, and a flexible pipe running down to the lucky 'showeree'. Considering such, shall we say, unique facilities, the pricing for my accommodation was, I thought, ambitious. Even enveloped in such a pristine environment, certain basic amenities are what visitors pay for. However, I marveled at a place, in the middle of exquisite nowhere, with no meals or piped water, but with an excellent wi-fi signal!

My charming hosts, the elderly half-Lakota, Gerald Weasel, and the full-blood Elmerilita Whiteface, who speaks only broken English, explain that their ancestors were from Crazy Horse's band but not of his family. That family, now surnamed Clown (since they are 'heyoka', the traditional holy jesters, commanded by the Thunder Beings to do, and say, everything in reverse or in a clownish manner), live in the hills around here. Gerald confirmed what I had read, that not even the family know just where in these Black Hills the great Crazy Horse lies buried.

Over an alleged breakfast of a tepid cup of coffee and a "Potato Ole Scrambler" (I am not a fan of pseudo-Mexican food, I discovered), I chatted with my hosts about what Bray calls "the clipped horizons of Reservation life." Living in one of the poorest places in the Western Hemisphere, he was despondent about the extensive corruption in tribal government. Later, at another place, I would hear how much good work this same tribal government is doing. By the end of my trip, I was unsure whether the tribal government is good or bad, though I suspect the reality lies, as it usually does, somewhere in the middle. Recalling my experience getting to them yesterday, I asked about Reservation roads or, sometimes, the lack of them. He explained that the main, black-topped roads on the Rez are Federal, with "US" designators; primary roads have "BIA" designators and are the responsibility of the Bureau of Indian Affairs; secondary roads also looked after by the BIA, are graded or gravel. From there to people's homes in the interiors, they are invariably dirt, with deep, muddy ruts, probably the responsibility of God – though He, clearly, has declined the honor.

Settling back into my little Ford, I panic to find my beloved Garmin in tantrum mode, refusing to switch on. My phone and iPad are also gradually dying in misery, as their adapters refuse to befriend the Reservation plugs. I am reduced to relying on my good old paper maps. Ah, well...the troubles of the road warrior. Fingers crossed, I head out, down the rutted, dusty, God-disavowed interior Reservation road, onto US-87, through gorgeous low, green hills. Over the weeks, I had noticed that, as the temperatures gradually dropped, moving north, so the price of gas inched up. I wondered if there is a correlation. Small, generally poor, wooden cottages, a few clearly more prosperous than others, most with multiple carcasses of deceased vehicles in their front yards (the initial skeletons for the famous "Rez cars"), dot the Reservation. My destination looked no different.

By now, the cheery morning had retreated in the face of threatening banks of towering, black clouds, spreading a grim overcast across the landscape. They seemed a perfect, Wagnerian background to my somber mood as I drove towards the ill-fated site of the Wounded Knee Massacre – the worst butchery of defenseless civilians by the US Army in its entire history, till My Lai in Vietnam. As I stepped reverentially onto the brooding lea beside the dry Wounded Knee Creek, the many little wisps of mist still enshrouding the land seemed like ghosts of Chief Big Foot's ragged, starving band of Miniconjou and Hunkpapa Lakota, trudging wearily in their pitiful rags across the freezing, snowbound landscape, under a huge white flag, desperately seeking safety and sustenance at the Red Cloud Agency in Pine Ridge. It was 29th December 1890, and the band comprised mainly women, children and the elderly, led by a mortally ill Chief.

Just weeks earlier, the towering legend, the revered Hunkpapa Wicasa Wakan, Holy Man, Chief Sitting Bull, Tatanka Yotanka, living a peaceful life on the Standing Rock Reservation had been ordered arrested by the infamous General Nelson Miles egged on by the unscrupulous Agent, James McLaughlin, who was deeply envious of the respect and regard universally accorded Sitting Bull. He insinuated, completely untruthfully, that Sitting Bull was encouraging the Ghost Dances which, he claimed, were preparations for war. Ironically, the Ghost Dance, created by the Piuate, Wovoka was, in reality, quite Christian in its tenets if not rituals, preaching love and non-violence leading to a reunion with family and loved ones in a more beneficent hereafter; in effect, a desperate people's yearning for survival. Sitting Bull had never taken part in, or supported, the Ghost Dances but he had been systematically humiliated and stripped of authority by the corrupt Agent who, like most of his ilk, had rapidly transformed into a petty tyrant once he overcame his paralyzing fear of his illustrious resident. Sitting Bull's people resisted this unjust arrest and, in the melee, the great Hunkpapa Chief, the last to give up arms, was shot in the back by Lakota policemen, a fate eerily similar to that of his friend and fellow warrior, Crazy Horse. The nearby town of McLaughlin still commemorates this shameful Agent.

Fearing a major disturbance after this assassination, two hundred of his people fled to the Miniconjou Chief, Big Foot (also known as Spotted Eagle) at Cheyenne River and together, they were racing desperately for sanctuary with Red Cloud. Just a fortnight after Sitting Bull's murder, near Porcupine Butte, the 7th Cavalry under Colonel Forsyth intercepted the refugees and guided them to camp at Wounded Knee, even having his Doctor tend to the dying Chief.

The following morning, the 350 starving, destitute Lakota woke to find themselves surrounded by over 500 troops, 22 artillerymen armed with four deadly Hotchkiss machine guns mounted on strategic rises around the camp, and 30 Native Scouts. What triggered the shooting remains unclear, but when the sun set that inauspicious day, 300 Lakota lay dead, including over 200 old women and children. The berserk soldiers' friendly fire even killed 25 of their own. They viewed this as the revenge of the 7th Cavalry for their humiliating defeat at the Little Bighorn – despite these Lakota not being anywhere near it and being obviously non-combatants. Heaping further infamy on themselves, the soldiers savagely mutilated and scalped the bodies, including that of the peace-advocating Chief Big Foot. Soldiers chased fleeing women and children as far as two miles and slaughtered them in cold blood, scalping their privates to display as trophies. Days later, the frozen bodies were dumped into a mass grave on a knoll covered in fading poverty grass, overlooking Wounded Knee Creek.

The theatre Commander, the notorious General Nelson Miles, saw nothing wrong in the encounter. The subsequent Army Court of Enquiry merely criticized Colonel Forsyth mildly but did not consider the massacre of innocent, defenseless civilians merited any punitive action.

The Pine Ridge Agent, the exceptional Dr. Valentin McGillycuddy, a rare good-hearted man, resigned in outrage, writing disgustedly to General Colby about the white settlers' false alarms inciting this massacre, "I neglected to state that, up to date, there has been neither a Sioux outbreak nor war. No citizen...has been killed, molested or can show the scratch of a pin, and no property been destroyed."

The 4 men and 47 women and children who survived were roughly dragged to Pine Ridge, and dumped in the freezing snow for long hours, before being herded into the nearby Episcopal Church – under a Christmas banner, "Peace on earth and goodwill to men".

Among the survivors was a child, a cousin of Crazy Horse, who would grow up to become the great seer, Black Elk. Towards the end of his life, looking back on that dread day, he summed it best, with profound melancholy, "I did not know then how much was ended...I can see that something else died there in the bloody mud and was buried in the blizzard. A people's dream died there...the Nation's hoop is broken and scattered.... the sacred tree is dead."

For this action, the county awarded the Army a remarkable 20 Congressional Medals of Honour. One citation even read "For conspicuous bravery in rounding up...a stampeded pack mule". Despite many calls for their revocation, these shameful awards still stand, to the country's continuing dishonor. Even the usually inhuman General Nelson Miles expressed mild unhappiness about this 'battle'.

The next day, the same unit of the 7th Cavalry headed out to round up (phraseology seemingly applied to both Longhorns and Natives) a few surviving Lakota who had escaped. Cornered at Clay Creek, these few harried warriors managed to so completely pin them down that they had to be rescued by the Buffalo Soldiers of the 9th Cavalry. This was the last splutter of the Lakota flame, a final testimony to their fighting spirit and valor.

Distressingly, these days, the field at Wounded Knee is ringed with fraud. Stalls peddling allegedly hand-made Lakota craft, usually shoddy kitsch from China, have sprung up with several people posing as chiefs or descendants of the victims to ease a few dollars out of gullible tourists. Among these, I met a pretty Lakota girl, Emerald Elk, who said she had an Indian (from India) teacher in her school in Pine Ridge. I was not sure if this was a new, empathic ploy to prise the lucre out of my sweaty fingers. Sadly, I wonder at a tribal government that ignores such a depressing desecration of hallowed ground.

Across the road, on the small hillock, is the mass grave where the victims were dumped by contractors hired by the Cavalry, having been left to rot and be desecrated by wild animals for two days. I make my way slowly to the red and white striped gate, surmounted by a Christian cross, though none of the victims were of the faith. While the hill is still in use as a community graveyard, the mass grave, in the center, is fenced off for some protection. A few forlorn little ribbons of cloth flutter in the slight breeze, each a heartfelt prayer tied to the fence by genuine descendants of the victims who come to pray over the remains of their long-departed relatives. As I gaze on this deeply melancholy sight, I am quietly greeted by Mike Yellowhorse. He is a full-blood Lakota and a volunteer with the Descendants Society, which is trying to protect and preserve the area of the mass grave, despite a crippling lack of funds or equipment. He points to the little Community Centre that they have built, a little downhill from the mass grave, but laments that much more is needed to do justice to this portentous place. He hopes, one day, there will be a museum here to tell the true story of what befell his people. For now, he and his family and friends try to guard the site against the fraudsters and vandals.

As we wander among the silent graves, he explains that the Lakota are still mainly full-bloods but, sadly, these days their young have little interest in their heritage and most cannot even speak their language.

While some effort is now being made to revive it, he, too, is bitter about the corruption endemic in tribal government. "The chiefs get themselves elected only to embezzle funds. They live the high life, and once even held a regular meeting of the tribal government in Las Vegas!"

He has a poor view of the militant American Indian Movement (AIM) too and feels they are nothing but troublemakers. Mike confirmed that alcohol and substance abuse are a problem among some (but, by no means, the majority) of the young. This is hardly unexpected among those who have lost their unusually intensive, generations-deep moorings in their heritage.

Deep in mid-winter, every year since 1986, a 191-mile Chief Big Foot Memorial Ride on horseback is held, recreating his trek from the Standing Rock Reservation to Wounded Knee, to keep alive the memory of the sacrifice of those who have walked on. The riders offer prayers and remembrances as they travel and, these days, they are frequently joined by many non-Natives, also paying homage.

Though the efforts of the European settlers, the US Army and the buffalo hunters seemed to have finally obliterated the proud

Lakota, they would rise again. And Wounded Knee would play a significant role one more time.

A century-old cry for justice reverberated through this valley in February 1973, when two hundred Oglala Lakota of the American Indian Movement seized Wounded Knee and faced off against five hundred heavily armed Federal Marshalls, supported by armored vehicles and even fighter jets, in a tense, 71-day armed stand-off, to draw attention to the Government's many dishonored treaties. Declassified documents now reveal that the 6th Army even considered a full-scale assault on Wounded Knee by Colonel Warner and the 82nd Airborne. The FBI covered itself in ignominy, making an Agreement with 'Tricky' Dick Wilson, the then tribal head, to give his goon squads immunity from arrest if they broke the law in trying to kill, not capture, AIM supporters. Frustrated US Marshals, unable to dislodge the AIM warriors, repeatedly machine-gunned a small, hapless pony that wandered in. TIME magazine's slightly mocking reportage revealed how little attitudes have changed. AIM warriors threatened by an overwhelming force of American troops had an eerie echo of Chief Big Foot's band encircled by Forsythe's machine guns, at this very place. The founder of AIM, Russell Means, is dead but his movement lives on, though sometimes considered controversial by those it seeks to serve, who often see it as bringing further grief to a desperate people. Whatever their mistakes, the warrior spirit of AIM undoubtedly restored a measure of pride and identity.

Much was made of AIM flying an upside-down US flag at Wounded Knee but, as Russell Means explained later, that is a well-known distress signal for people in trouble. The Natives certainly were. Still are.

Driving pensively away from melancholy Wounded Knee, I recalled the 1890 comment in South Dakota's Saturday Pioneer, "Having wronged them for centuries, we had better, in order to protect our civilization, follow it up by one more wrong and wipe these untamed and untameable creatures from the face of the earth."

Some elements of the Army had, clearly, decided to.

Just 15 miles down the road from Pine Ridge, a few scant miles from where I would turn off tomorrow, at Tobacco Road, lies the little town of Oglala, home to a mainly 'traditionalist' community of Lakota. Exactly two years after the stand-off at Wounded Knee, a small AIM group was encamped there when two FBI agents stormed in and threatened them with automatic rifles. Their foolhardy position, out in the open facing a group armed to defend itself, made it obvious that they expected rapid reinforcement by the massive law-enforcement team that had quietly surrounded the camp. Their objective was to kill, not capture, the AIM leadership there. However, as usual, the Natives held off the 'cavalry', and the two FBI Agents provocateurs died. Despite being completely ringed by an overwhelming force of FBI, US Marshals and BIA Police, by land, air, and river, all but one of the AIM warriors escaped.

A massive manhunt followed across the US and Canada, but the FBI had already decided which AIM leader they wanted to pin everything on. Using a stunningly disreputable mix of forged affidavits, coerced witnesses who were not, blatant falsehood, and some unabashedly racist Midwest judges, the FBI finally extradited Leonard Peltier from Canada and convict him, despite clear evidence that he had not shot the Agents. To this day, a decade and a half later, he remains incarcerated in a maximum security facility, despite worldwide appeals for a pardon.

The only hopeful incident in this sordid FBI campaign against AIM and the Natives occurred in the town of Cedar Rapids, Iowa, where some AIM leaders were tried. Normally a traditional, conservative, anti-Native town, it became even more so with the influx of a large group of AIM supporters. However, the behavior of the AIM group was so exemplary, with no alcohol or violence, while they talked to the townsfolk to explain who they were, what had happened to them, and how they were only seeking justice, that the tide turned. The people were so completely won over that they joined the AIM supporters wholeheartedly in demanding justice at the trial. This storybook turn of sentiment undoubtedly influenced the jury, since the two leaders received a very rare acquittal.

Though this, the second-largest Reservation in America, is larger than Delaware and Rhode Island combined, with an estimated population of 40,000 Lakota, it had originally been far larger. Relentlessly incited by greedy settlers and unscrupulous missionaries alike, the Federal Government, in far off Washington enacted the General Allotment Act in 1889, to break up communally held tribal lands into individual tracts, destroying the very basis of tribal society and culture, and declared the large, unallocated acres "excess," handing them over to, naturally, white settlers. Coincidentally, those "excess acres" always turned out to be the most prime.

These are the hungry lands, with 80% unemployment, 49% below the Federal poverty line, infant mortality five times the national average, and a life expectancy that is the lowest in the entire Western Hemisphere. Obesity, diabetes, and heart disease are almost epidemics, with health care well below acceptable levels in the country. Despite all this, sadly, less than 1% of all charities, annually, go to benefit Native Americans. Such is the desolate plight today of those who once were the undisputed Lords of the Plains.

Pine Ridge itself is essentially a collection of villages, comprised of the usual wooden cottages. A few decaying businesses in rigor mortis, long abandoned by customers and hope, lie scattered among the living. I finally located a Taco John for a quick bite to eat. The only other eatery I could see was a Pizza Hut which was closed, perhaps permanently. While digging into my frugal meal, I could finally plug my phone and iPad in to charge before delving deeper into the Rez.

My next port of call was the nearby Red Cloud Indian Mission School, reputed to have an interesting Heritage Centre. As advised by their website, I had emailed in advance, requesting the proffered tour. It also has the grave of Red Cloud. I was ashiver with expectation. Just a short drive from Pine Ridge on the excellent road, the old mission school was easy to find. It turned out that, of all days, I had chosen the one on which they were busy celebrating the 50th anniversary of their Summer Art Show. Whatever artifacts and heritage items there might once have been, had been removed; presumably artsy people were milling about everywhere; the staff, hardly any of whom appeared to be Native, were distracted and not particularly helpful, only able to point me towards the gift shop. Nobody had any idea about the promised tour.

This was very disappointing, especially as I had emailed in advance, requesting an interview with their Director of Curriculum, Najiu Clifford, excited by his online comment, "So often the narrative of the Pine Ridge Reservation is that of deep and immense poverty, of incredible violence or sadness. But Red Cloud is a pocket of hope. I think that's exactly what we provide here, hope for the future, and the tools in order for our students to open those doors."

I would have loved to explore that thought further with its author.

Clearly, their website is a piece of snappy marketing. I found almost nothing of historical interest there. For a school founded by Red Cloud, this was surprising. The School has always been run by Jesuits and, in trying to locate parking, I found slots "Reserved for Jesuits," something I have not seen even at the Vatican. The School's tuition is just $100 a year, but unaffordable for many Lakota parents. Fortunately, as many as 600 young Lakota do receive a sound, if Christianity-saturated, Jesuit-slanted education. I would have liked to learn, from the educators, whether the worldview imparted to these young minds is a Lakota-centric one or the old Euro-centric bias on display in the period photographs in the School's 'historical' gallery.

Red Cloud, Mahapiya Luta, the once awe-inspiring warrior, and statesman was never elected a Chief by the Oglala of the northern Plains. However, his relentless war, to prevent settlers from flooding onto the Bozeman Trail and destroying their life-sustaining hunting grounds, fought the US Army to a complete standstill over two years and is usually enshrined in history as "Red Cloud's War", the most successful outcome against the US Army till Vietnam. The resultant Fort Laramie Treaty is the only recognition of unconditional defeat ever signed by the US Government in its entire history. It was the zenith of his career and his life, so full of contradictions and contrary behaviors. So successful was his campaign of attrition that the Army eventually retreated from the entire Powder River Valley, abandoning all their Forts on the Bozeman Trail to be systematically burnt to the ground by Red Cloud's warriors.

Among them was the young Crazy Horse, beginning to learn the warcraft in which he would overshadow them all. A highly successful war leader, Red Cloud, had, like Crazy Horse, appreciated early the need to move from individual fights for honor, to ordered, larger-scale battles. At some point though, along with Crazy Horse's Maternal Uncle, Spotted Tail, he realized that the tide had turned inexorably against the Lakota. A visit to Washington D.C. and New York, where the so-called 'Great Father' went to some pains to impress them with a demonstration of the Army's artillery firepower, reinforced this conviction. The canny Red Cloud quickly smoked the peace pipe and turned to politics, soon winning an Agency of his own.

Where his own people declined to make him Chief, the wasicu did, at last finding someone of stature who could be molded to their wishes. His considerable prestige as a war leader frittered away into Reservation trivialities over the coming years, and he found his authority eroded by both Agents and his own people. Compounded by blindness in his last years, he became a disappointed man, bitterly jealous of the continued respect and renown of Crazy Horse, who had continued a heroic fight against the invaders while Red Cloud morphed into an Agency politician of uncertain integrity. There is considerable controversy over his murky role in the murder of his imagined rival. Unclear if his hand was bloodied with the final act, in some manner, there is no doubt he successfully set the stage for it by falsely poisoning General Crook against the, by then, peaceful Crazy Horse. Though in later years many condemned him for becoming more a politician than a statesman, he did undoubtedly gain peace for his people. As a result, he is among the very few war chiefs who died peacefully of old age.

As Cindy Catches would put it tomorrow, with gentle diplomacy, "Red Cloud and Crazy Horse represented two different views of life."

As I walked up a little hill, to the cemetery overlooking the valley and the School he set up, I could see the redoubtable warhorse's grave from afar, set slightly apart. Standing over it, I ruminated on the life of this remarkable, if sometimes controversial, man. I also wondered at the Christian cross placed over the grave of the man who once said, about Christ, "We have seen neither Him nor His Works."

Bibles and bullets have been the tried and trusted remedy of Western colonizers through the ages.

Next to his relatively magnificent grave, is the small, rather neglected grave of his wife, with a worn, weather-beaten, wooden cross for a headstone, part of her name worn away by the elements. It is a peculiarly disrespectful lack of maintenance for the final resting place of the founder's spouse.

Clockwise from top left: Author's Tepee-on-the-Prairie; the lonely hilltop mass grave at Wounded Knee; the indomitable Stella Iron Cloud; the grave of Red Cloud (note his wife's humble grave beside his); Peter Catches' sacred Sun Dance Tree; Cindy & Peter Catches with Author.

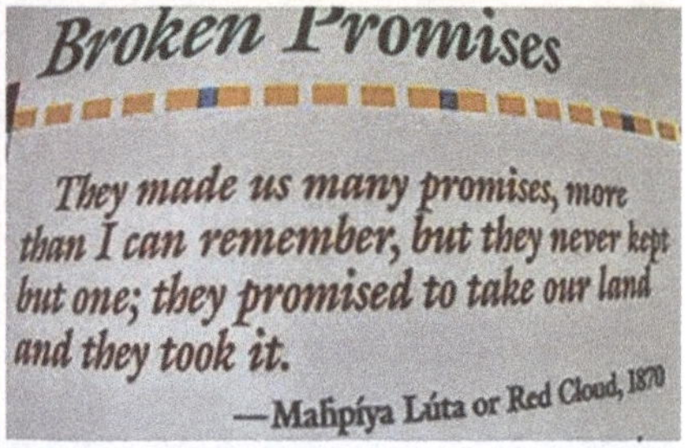

Clockwise from top: Mark St. Pierre at his fledgling film school on the Pine Ridge Reservation; sad but true words of Red Cloud; approaching the Badlands; the delightful Odd Duck Inn of the St. Pierre's; Medicine Wheel Garden at the Akta Lakota Museum, Chamberlain.

DAY 14 : 3 JUNE - THE LAST MEDICINE MAN

Disaster! My phones and iPad are again out of juice, and my little tepee has no electricity. My treasured Garmin sulkily refuses to switch on this morning too. As icing on the cake, my phone has not picked up any network at all on the Reservation (or even in Dodge City, come to think of it). Finally, later that morning, my video camera abruptly shut down just two minutes into my interview with Cindy Catches. On yet another beautiful, cold morning (8 Celsius, though it feels much colder), with birds joyously celebrating the lush verdure all around, my day just keeps getting sadder!

I drift from war to spirituality, as I maneuver cautiously down the deeply rutted, muddy Tobacco Road, to meet with a real-life, hereditary Wicasa Wakan, holy Medicine Man, of the Lakota. There is something apt about heading to a spiritual discussion along "Tobacco Road" since tobacco is an essential part of every Native religious ceremony. Smoked out of a pipestone-bowl pipe, it represents the lifeblood of the people. I have been corresponding for months with Cindy Catches, wife of Peter V. Catches, to set up an interview that I know in my bones would be one of the real highlights of my entire journey. There was considerable uncertainty about this happening at all, as Peter is seriously ill and not expected to live. As I continue along that well-furrowed track, I pray I will be privileged to speak with him before he traveled to the "other side."

Though dressed in jeans and a T-shirt Peter, following in the footsteps of his father, Petaga Yuha Mani or Pete Catches, is the deeply respected 38th Medicine Man of his people, keeper of the way of the Spotted Eagle, one of the highest medicine levels. The calling of a Medicine Man arises from one's innermost spirit and is not necessarily hereditary. His maternal grandfather was a survivor of Wounded Knee, while his great grandmother was the sister of Black Shawl, the wife of Crazy Horse. Cindy is white, a Baha'i from West Virginia who has spent a lifetime imbibing the wisdom of the Holy Medicine Man and watching him perform cures that defy conventional medicine. Together, they have set up Oceti Wakan, the Sacred Fireplace, to institutionalize their lore. I know the very elderly Peter Catches His Enemy, Zintkala Oyate, is dying, but he is happy to talk with me, sitting beside Cindy, occasionally elucidating on her comments, looking searchingly into my very soul. Despite his extreme frailty, he displays flashes of quiet humor.

Native Americans have always been supreme masters of the spirit world, just as Westerners are of the material. First, she explains the importance of tobacco to the Way of the Pipe. Native tobacco, canasta, is the inner bark of the willow and is not meant to be smoked like leaf tobacco. The puffs of fragrant smoke from the Sacred Pipe travel up to the Great Spirit and establish a mystical link for prayer. Many elements of their faith, as I had already observed, bear striking resemblances to core Hindu philosophy, Shinto and, probably, Baha'i. The Hindu 'yugs' echo the Navajo belief that we are living through the 5th age of man. Unlike Euro-centric man-created God imagery, Natives use direct observation of Nature and natural forces to focus their spirituality. They shy away from all-knowing prophecies and humbly accept that there are many unknowns, even unknowable, about the Great Mystery. There is no 'him' or 'her' to the Great Spirit. Like the Hindus, the Lakota not only believe in the existence of a spirit world on the "other side," but also in a concept similar to 'karma' wherein all one's deeds in this life add up, good and bad and, unlike Christian belief, they cannot be selectively forgiven through confession or tithe. Memories cannot be altered. The Celtics had a similar belief until the tsunami of Christianity overwhelmed them. Beneath the surface, Native communities continue to be profoundly different from the dominant culture.

Where Semitic religions are based on fear, with an invented Devil, Natives believe in fearlessness to walk the Red Road of goodness and virtue. They never proselytize or convert. There is considerable irony in that the European colonizers, the supreme materialists, forced their religion on the supreme spiritualists, claiming an absolute monopoly of the knowledge of the One Big Spirit. One cannot help but recall that, despite their arrogant spiritual hegemony, every one of their hundreds of broken, dishonored treaties were signed, "In God we trust."

I asked the Catches about the Medicine Wheel, a circle of four colored quadrants. While it has many levels of meaning and symbolism, broadly, Green represents the physical world, extolling virtue and generosity; Red symbolizes the emotional world, exalting courage and caring; Yellow is for the spiritual world, and its virtue is fidelity, first to Wakan Tanka, the Great Mystery, and then to one's family and people; White reflects the mental dimension and fortitude. The Red Road is the way of good deeds, virtue, positivity, peace, love, and wisdom. The Black Road is the path of conflict, hardship, discord, and difficulty. I explained to them that, despite my very limited understanding, I am striving with the utmost humility, to tread the Red Road on my pilgrimage – though I glimpse the Black Road now and then. They both smile in serene understanding.

As the supreme skeptic, I question Peter on the motivation behind Lakota religious practices, and he quietly reminds me that their rituals are, primarily, for holistic healing. Medicine Man is a more accurate job description of the Wicasa Wakan, than Holy Man. And their cures have repeatedly worked. After all, as he puts it, "Nature is God, God is Nature."

Authentic Medicine Men do not accept money, nor any personal or political advantage, for the service they provide. They embed the entire value system in virtue, love, the wholeness of the spirit, service and, in a very Shinto way, being one with Nature. Mother Earth, Father Sky and the four cardinal directions (which also have multiple levels of meaning) are at the core of their beliefs. The strength of this tradition is attested to by the fact that, despite several generations of forced conversion and brutal attempts to remake them in the image of the invaders, there is now a reversal of that flow, back to Wakan Tanka and the Way of the Pipe. As Clyde Warrior, a Ponca youth leader, puts it, "...if there is one thing that characterizes Indian life today, it is poverty of the spirit."

However, that is slowly changing, and there is a clear move back to Wakan Tanka.

Ironically, the US Government, and countries around the world, frequently invite Peter to advise them on Native holistic healing – the same Government that severely punished any practice of Native religion till as late as 1979. Lately, the Catches have developed – in a strange twist of fate, under a grant from the Federal Government – a graduated curriculum of lessons on Lakota spirituality, "Life Skills for the Young Lakota", to be taught to Native children over years, to help them reclaim their culture. Cindy estimates that there are less than 6000 fluent Lakota speakers left, mainly elderly, and the language is in extreme danger of extinction. The role of generational trauma in the high rates of suicide and substance abuse among the young is only now beginning to be understood. DNA analyses have recently revealed the deep, long-term damage inflicted by generational trauma and the healing effects of ceremonial practices. Peter confirms that they have even cured cancer, though it requires one to rid oneself of all thoughts of anger, jealousy, envy and such negative emotions, a state of mind difficult to attain that can take up to six months to achieve. Cindy explains that children are innocent, without knowledge, so the missionary schools tried to indoctrinate them into believing the Medicine Man is the Devil's henchman, and that it is their fault that their heritage is intrinsically evil, in every way. The child, thus deeply wounded in spirit, grows up to eventually discover the truth, leading to a mind fractured by their early conditioning.

Peter is tiring fast and needs to sleep. Before he goes to bed, I ask a final, very personal question, "Why have I felt such a strange, powerful passion for the Lakota for a half-century, from a world away?"

Peter smiles, "I know you don't believe it, but perhaps you were one of us in an earlier life."

As I sadly watch him go in, I know I will never see him again. I had so much more to ask. Unfortunately, I do not believe in reincarnation or an afterlife. Perhaps there just is no explanation; perhaps it's one of the "more things in heaven and earth than are dreamt of in your philosophy" kind of thing. Perhaps it's just my pathetic poverty of spirit, now so clear to me.

Cindy and I continue talking on the patio of their little cottage, amid the chatter of birds and the buzzing of bees in the shrubbery. She reminisces about meeting Martin Luther King Jr., and their efforts, along with twenty tribes in Tennessee, to build a multi-cultural, multi-faith center which would also propagate Native holistic healing. She explains, one has to look beyond the color of the skin because, if a part of humanity is hurt, it affects all of it. We are all related to each other and to all natural things around us. Mitakuye oyasin.

She confirms that there is still very strong and widespread prejudice against Natives, especially against the less integrated, full-bloods of the Northern Plains. It is considerably worse than the prejudice against African Americans, though less visible. Cindy feels this is because many whites are the descendants of those who stole the land, and some cope with this inherited guilt through offense as a defense. Cindy postulates, "The Government is making life very difficult on the Reservation, hoping to force people away. Then they can take over the land, the only thing we have left, and, essentially, finish the job of making the Indians disappear. Then they will not have to look in the mirror anymore and remember what they did."

In a bizarre perversion of history, where, a century ago, they brutally forced the Natives onto restricted Reservations, now the efforts are on to drive them off the Reservations. Now, instead of military might, it is through economic strangulation.

I ask about support from the Federal Government and she replies, "It does honor the treaties to provide healthcare, housing, and education, but the quality is the poorest in the country – much like the rotten goods provided as annuities a century ago. For example, they spend $3000 a year on a Reservation school, against $6000 in the rest of the country."

After a pause, she chuckles, "Did you know that the Bureau of Indian Affairs was under the Secretary of War, and that they set it up with no authorization from Congress?"

The vision of Crazy Horse had prophesied this generation would bring about the revival of the Lakota. The Medicine Man's words and deeds, simply cannot be dismissed, restoring the comfortable certainties my logic-shackled, skeptic soul had basked in all these years. Perhaps this road-trip is turning into more of a voyage of self-discovery than I had bargained for.

As I get into my car, to visit his nearby Sun Dance Tree of Life, Peter's sister-in-law runs out and hands me a small, dry, wild turnip, "Peter would like you to keep this with you. It is very sacred to us."

Just five days later, on 8th June, Cindy informed me that Peter had passed to the "other side", to join the grandfathers. My photographs were the last ones of him. I would never have another opportunity to benefit from his wisdom – and wit. Pila Maya, thank you, Peter Catches His Enemy. He was not the last Medicine Man, but the last Medicine Man of his ilk. The Earth may not know his like again.

DAY 15: 4 JUNE - INVISIBLE WARRIORS

Invisible warriors! This is Reservation author and filmmaker, Mark St. Pierre's brilliantly evocative name for the unsung individuals fighting unbelievable odds to improve the lives of their people on the Pine Ridge Reservation. It has taken me to my last day "on Rez" to discover this intensely passionate, unabashedly idiosyncratic, "troublemaker-activist" and his equally talented, full-blood Lakota descendant of Chief American Horse, educationist & celebrated craftsperson wife, Tilda. A Master Traditional Artist, whose quillwork, beadwork and dolls feature in many collections around the country, she founded Cloud Horse in 2001, still a rare Native arts and cultural organization on a Reservation.

Sadly, even such a pioneering venture receives zero State or Federal support. Mark is a Canadian meiti – part Native, part French (heritage of the early fur trappers, who frequently settled into Native tribes), with a mad flourish of Irish to top it off. Despite the choice of living almost anywhere in the world, and having operated a successful Native art gallery in Steamboat Springs, Colorado, the couple moved back "on Rez" over 26 years ago, despite the continuing, severe discrimination they face from white America. Yesterday, leaving the Catches in a thoughtful and deeply pensive mood, I had driven past Wounded Knee, through Sharp's Corner towards Kyle. Heading past the Oglala Lakota College, I had turned down American Horse Road towards Red Owl Springs to get to the St. Pierres' delightful little Odd Duck Inn.

Waking from a very comfortable night at the cosy little Inn, under the usual crisp 16 Celsius skies, eating a great breakfast cooked by my fascinating host, Mark, it dawns on me that each district of the Pine Ridge Reservation has its own character – the Manderson-Wounded Knee area, for instance, is more depressed, hopeless and on the lookout for hand-outs, while the Kyle-Porcupine area is much more prosperous, with successful farms, ranches, and businesses. I saw several tractors at work out in the fields and no signs of the rotting carcasses of any deceased businesses. One such successful enterprise is the excellent Lakota Prairie Ranch Resort, where the traditional, warm-hearted friendliness of the Lakota is on full display. I had the pleasure of hosting Mark and Tilda for dinner here, over a fascinating conversation ("Of course we'll come! Ever heard of a Lakota refusing food?"). Apparently, the tribal government had, at one time, tried to move to Kyle from Pine Ridge, but locals refused and used the earmarked land to set up the Oglala Lakota College, instead. Mark was the first Executive Director of the Pine Ridge Area Chamber of Commerce, next door. Its first meeting had just three members – Mark, Tilda, and Sissy Patton. Mark has been something of a serial entrepreneur on the Reservation, trying (unsuccessfully, on that occasion) to set up the very first credit union in Native America. He is a passionate (very!) advocate for the Lakota standing on their own feet and not depending on uncertain exterior help, unhesitatingly putting his own money where his mouth is.

Although more than half the population now lives and works "off Rez," and the rest, mainly the elderly, have a very limited ability to improve their lives, Mark sees a definite revival of Lakota values and pride in their identity. There is a significant improvement in Lakota-oriented education and a surge back to Native spirituality. That most Christian churches are largely empty these days is mute testimony to this, as so brilliantly portrayed in his documentary film, "Who Will Bury the Dead?" I saw the truth of this gradual revival myself, even in my few short days on the Reservation.

Unfortunately, everything still flows from nearby Rapid City and the Lakota have to spend most of their very limited, hard-earned dollars there, as even the necessities of life, and medical care, are rarely available on the Rez. So, the Federal Government's Treaty money eventually ends up back in the hands of the wasicu. Conversely, it also means that Rapid City's economy heavily depends on Pine Ridge and the other Reservations nearby, giving it a large vested interest in ensuring that the lack of development on the Reservations continues. Hence the lack of banks, car dealerships, insurance offices, realtors, large grocery stores, big-box retailers and suchlike, and this is likely to continue – unless the Lakota tribal government does something about it themselves. They have already made a beginning, with the establishment of – what else! – two very successful casino resorts on the Reservation. In 1976, it sued the Federal Government over water rights and won, resulting in 90% of the population on the Reservation now having access to good, piped water. Tribal Council meetings these days are broadcast live on TV, sharply improving accountability and the quality of governance. This, unintentionally, reflects the ancient tradition of Native American Council Lodges, which were open on all sides so anyone in the tribe could sit around and listen in on the discussions of the leaders. Another major contributing factor to the recent sharp improvement in the quality of tribal governance is the fact that today fully half the council, and the police, are women. A far cry from the days of the corrupt Chairman Richard Wilson and his appositely acronym-ed GOON (Guardians Of the Oglala Nation) squad, one of the sparks that ignited the AIM Wounded Knee confrontation.

Tribal revenues, however, are still mainly Federal treaty monies channeled through various programs including a share of the income from the Badlands National Park. Deprived of civil society for over a century, they are still deprived of participation in supply economics, condemned to remaining buyers and consumers rather than makers or traders, continuing the drain of wealth and the perpetuation of poverty on the Reservation. Efforts towards self-reliance need to continue strongly, especially now that there is a whole generation of college-educated professionals available.

The paucity of development funds and the discrimination of mainstream bankers are major constraints. Though a Lakota Community Development Fund was created in Kyle, the first of its kind in Native America, whose object is specifically to support Native American businesses, the obvious predicament that most do not have the equity to guarantee loans means that no loans are actually disbursed despite the facility existing, on paper. When US Attorney General, Janet Reno, successfully sued a bank in Martin for discrimination against Native Americans, they complied with the Court's directive to extend banking facilities to the Reservation by sending in a small mobile unit, with restricted services, for just 5 hours a week, satisfying the letter of the law though profaning its spirit.

I am staying at another venture of the dynamic St. Pierres, the Odd Duck Inn. Commenting on that effort, he smiled wryly, "Do you know there is not a single bank on the Reservation? We have to go to Rapid City for everything. Even for Odd Duck Inn, they forced us to pay a shocking 9.5% interest."

Unlike most places on the Reservation, Mark has clearly signposted the way to the Inn, and I had no difficulty finding my way there, despite it being a bit into the interior, off any remotely beaten track. Having arrived, I knocked on the door of the B&B and was met with peaceful silence. Scratching my head, I drove over to the house next door and hollered, only to hear more serene stillness. After standing around in a quandary for a while, I drove back to the B&B to try again, just in case someone had magically materialized. And he had! In the form of a genial, white-haired genie named Mark St. Pierre. With a warm welcome to their Odd Duck Inn, he showed me around the excellent little facility. It was, easily, the best accommodation I had seen on the Reservation with, as I would discover, the most congenial hosts conceivable. On the spot, I decided to return the following year with my wife. After the sixty seconds it took me to settle in, Mark and I chatted over a welcome cup of coffee that he brewed for me, with typical open-hearted hospitality. Mark and Tilda are a wellspring of local knowledge and expertise that I happily tapped into while, I like to think, it pleasantly surprised him to discover how deep and genuine my interest in the Lakota is. That conversation would open the door for me to gain a much more intimate look into the life of the Reservation than an outsider could normally have expected on such a short visit. I soon realized, with amusement, that Mark tries to cultivate the image of a grouchy old man, but the facade keeps slipping in the face of his ever kind, humane and gentle nature. But it is a worthy act – after all, he runs a film school!

Without being asked, Mark generously gave up most of his day to show me around, and gave me a rare, in-depth insight into Reservation life and how the invisible warriors are slowly transforming it to match its exquisite, pristine environment. Progress is admittedly very slow, but definitely discernible and growing. Young Lakota are finally starting to peel back the layers of trauma and confront it meaningfully to build a stronger future. When people have been deprived of civil society for well over a century, recovery cannot but take time. A visit to the Oglala Lakota College at Kyle is educative. Among other features, they have a memorial to all the Lakota veterans of the two World Wars and I was stunned to discover what an enormous number of them there were, something that one rarely hears about in mainstream America. Over 10,000 Native American soldiers died in WWI alone. America has rarely acknowledged its minority patriots, whether African American or Native American. Showing me around the College, Mark explains that the Lakota young have a very real hunger for knowledge. This College's graduation rates are higher than those of the whole State of South Dakota. Unfortunately, it is not always an easy road, as he narrates the story of an East European Lakota language teacher, hired by the College at considerable expense, fluent in the language but with absolutely no sensitivity to their culture or traditions, such as respect for tribal elders. His teaching, sadly, ended up more superficial than truly enriching for his students.

Visiting their fledgling film-making program, the Reel Jobs Film School, a part of their Cloud Horse Art Institute, I am astounded at how much they have achieved with just a small, initial USDA grant. Their documentary, "Who Will Bury the Dead?" is near Hollywood quality. For the students, often escaping alcohol-soaked homes or parents, the Studio is living proof of how far the Lakota will stretch their extremely hard-won dollars, wrested out of the sweaty grip of an unsupportive, and often deeply prejudiced, bureaucracy to achieve their dreams. Films are a powerful means of preserving the Lakota language and culture, to save them from extinction, and this nascent effort is as vital as a heartbeat.

The cracked windscreen and malfunctioning window of Mark's war-weary station-wagon evidence the St. Pierres' sheer grit and tenacity, channeling their own scant dollars to support their fledgling Lakota educational ventures in the face of extraordinary adversity. I see a similar passion in Tony Brave, who started what, at the time, was Native America's only TV station, almost two decades ago. His televising of Tribal Council meetings, for instance, has gone a long way to ensuring transparency and accountability in the community. A similar success story is the Reservation's Kili Radio, which I enjoy listening to on my drives around the Rez. But it still faces the deadly rip-tide of opposition from 'dominant society'. The Post Office at Kyle, for example, operates just 4 hours a day. Small wonder I missed my mailing for Cindy.

Where even a haircut was unavailable on the Reservation and watching a movie involved a two-hour expedition to Rapid City with a family outlay of around $200, now things are changing, almost rapidly. The new cinema at Kyle charges just $7 to enjoy the latest movies; convenience stores are emerging; over half the people at Pine Ridge Reservation now own their modest homes, debt-free; the tribal government is slowly beginning to improve roads and infrastructure – far more than was done under the Bureau of Indian Affairs which, for the longest time, had no Natives in it at all. Off-Reservation Natives, especially mixed-bloods, have little knowledge of life on the Reservations and tend to condescend. Traditional Natives are sometimes described, pejoratively, as "returning to the blanket." National media largely ignores them, as

I was to find to my utter exasperation, while international media, in the very rare instances they bother at all, prefer to focus on the usual sensationalist aspects of poverty, misery, substance abuse, the cheap stereotype of the lazy, drunk Indian. Nothing of their amazing success stories, their amazing fights against all the odds, their amazing, quiet resurgence. The reality, perhaps less media sensational, is that the Reservation is transforming itself in a quiet but remarkable manner despite stuntingly limited resources, in this forgotten nook of a massively resource-rich nation. They have afforded me a rare glimpse beyond the caricature.

Mark took me over to meet another remarkable person who immediately warmed my heart, someone who starred in his film, Stella Iron Cloud, a direct descendant of the renowned Santee Chief, Red Wing. She is elderly, in constant pain and wheelchair-restricted, but nothing diminishes her bubbling humor, warmth and sheer, infectious joie de vivre. With a booming, ready laugh that reveals her gusto for life, she really is the Undefeatable Stella Iron Cloud! She generously takes time to explain her invaluable genealogy work and shares stories of her ancestors, true Native royalty. One anecdote is about her grandmother taking her, as a little girl, to see the first movie to have Lakota dialogue in it and tell their story. Halfway through, just before a cavalry charge, her Grandmother abruptly pulled her out. When the disappointed Stella asked why, she replied, "I cannot bear to watch the Cavalry killing the Indians all over again." She had survived Wounded Knee as a small child, only to watch out-of-control soldiers rampage through Pine Ridge killing any survivors their whimsy chanced upon. Interestingly, the Principal of the Oglala Lakota College, Thomas Shortbull, is a direct descendent of Short Bull, who had falsely led the Lakota to believe their Ghost Dance Shirts could stop bullets, and so was at least partly culpable for Wounded Knee.

I asked Stella about the historical perspective of their people today, and she explained, with characteristic spirit, "The taunts and abuse of the boarding schools really brought home the ordeal of being transformed from the lords of the plains, as you put it, to a subservient, conquered people. But that doesn't mean you have to stay conquered and subservient."

Unsurprisingly, inherited trauma with its deep-rooted identity crisis is alive and flourishing among the deeply brutalized Lakota. The obsolescence of their traditional vocational skills, warfare, hunting, horse-breeding; their complete lack of training in new skills like farming and business, ensuring they could not even feed themselves, becoming utterly reliant on the wasicu's miserly dole; white missionaries forcibly taking their children away to boarding schools to indoctrinate and abuse them; the endless discrimination against them as "savage, lazy and drunk"; the near-total lack of jobs, education or prospects, all leading to a horrifyingly steep rate of suicide, depression, alcoholism and drug abuse – a self-fulfilling prophecy, born of utter hopelessness. It is only now, through the tireless efforts of the invisible warriors, that the tide has begun to turn. And turn sharply. Even in matters of land ownership. After the Federal Government broke the Reservation up into individual plots, many impoverished allottees ended up having to sell to unscrupulous settlers, resulting in nearly half the Reservation lands now being owned by outsiders. Now, the tribal government is gradually buying back many of those plots for the tribe – slowly repairing the societal and cultural devastation of the Dawes Act.

Thanks to the warm-hearted hospitality of Mark St. Pierre, today was the only day of my thirty-day odyssey that I did not drive a single kilometer. I have now covered two-thirds of my total mileage and half my total planned days on the road. As I return to Mark & Tilda's lovely Odd Duck Inn, amidst charming isolation, I ponder how much I have learned, how many preconceptions have changed, how emotions have been roiled. But, above all, how inspiring have been the stories of the undefeated heroes, the invisible warriors, a generation of educated professionals, now truly winning the West, their West, against inconceivable odds.

DAY 16: 5 JUNE - TO THE MISSOURI!

Another great breakfast prepared by Mark (despite his tongue-in-cheek poster, "Bed & Breakfast – you make both"), a final, long chat about their film school and other efforts, and I head out from the Odd Duck Inn with considerable reluctance. It has been illuminating and enjoyable, and, in hindsight, I wish I had planned a longer stay. Ah, well...

Passing the Oglala Lakota College, I stop for a quick peek at their Historical Museum, extolled by their website. It was small and sparse. Surely here, of all places, there should have been a rich vein of heritage and lore to tap into. I even noticed a minor error in one display, a photograph captioned "Man Afraid of His Horses". As they know perfectly well, the famous war chief was actually "Man Whose Enemies are Afraid Even of his Horses." I admit to feeling just a tad smug!

From the Pine Ridge Reservation, I entered the Rosebud Reservation, the erstwhile home of Crazy Horse's step maternal uncle, Spotted Tail, the man who, once his hero, mentor, and tutor in the arts of war, eventually denied him sanctuary when his life was threatened at the Red Cloud Agency. Spotted Tail, of all people, could not but have been well aware of the enduring modesty and humility of the man he had watched grow from infant to mystical legend. The Lakota follow a maternal lineage, and men were almost always closer to their maternal relatives than their paternal ones. Despite all the bonds of family and tradition, it was only his cousin from his birth mother's side, and close friend, Chief Touch the Clouds, who welcomed him with an open heart and stood staunchly by him to the tragic end.

The Rosebud Reservation, like Pine Ridge, is beautiful and verdant with gentle hills and I was glad I had driven most of the way through it rather than head straight onto the freeway. I marveled at the first blossoms of a hopeful future clear everywhere. As I drifted through the little towns, heading towards the border with nearby North Dakota, I got to thinking about the recent news of politics and disenfranchisement. In San Juan County in Utah, though the Navajo and Utes form the majority, the voting districts have been gerrymandered to guarantee an artificial majority representation for non-Natives, primarily whites.

In North Dakota, even worse shenanigans have ensured it remains a State with a dominant white vote, despite an overwhelming majority of Native Americans in the population. This was achieved by an innovative variety of blatantly disreputable actions - restricting the number of registration forms available on the Reservations, intimidating voters by locating polling booths inside Sheriffs' offices, denying polling locations on the Reservations, and the global favorites – running out of ballots, or the voting machines breaking down.

Jacqueline De Leon, a Pueblo attorney at the Native American Rights Fund, confirms, "Racism and discrimination exist to a degree that would be appalling to most Americans. The disenfranchisement is familiar, and the tools are familiar."

The latest tool, in North Dakota, is arbitrarily disallowing the vote to anyone with a Post Office Box address, which covers almost all Natives as there are hardly any physical postal addresses on the Reservations because of a lack of coverage by USPS. Besides being deprived of a voice within a democracy, this disenfranchisement has direct impacts – gerrymandering of voting districts, no new schools or roads, no language development help, no running water facilities, and more. Even Courts rarely select Natives for jury service. In Utah, for instance, Natives finally received the right to vote only in 1957, but the same year, the Bureau of Land Management forced many of them from their homes, pushing them away from white people and gerrymandering their voting districts.

Bruce Adams, a County Commission Chairman, brazenly claimed that "nobody had really settled in Utah" before the Mormons. Even more disgraceful was Republican County Commissioner, Phil Lyman, who claimed the Navajos "lost the war" and so should have no role in local land management. Fortunately, the slow, uphill fightback for their political rights is finally gaining momentum. Today, there are 64 Native members of State legislatures in 15 States and even 2 Congressmen. In the latest, 2018 mid-term elections, the two first-ever Native American women have been elected to the House of Representatives. It has been a long time coming.

Moving out of the Rosebud Reservation, onto I-90, I pass the tiny town of Wasta, bringing on a little chuckle. Back home, in Oman, the word 'wasta' means influence or having the connections to sway the powers that be. About fifty miles short of the Missouri, near Chamberlain, the road suddenly changed to a red surface that I had seen nowhere before. Now, I am literally on the red road! The gentle horseback motion over jointed concrete slabs, which I had become so used to over the past few weeks, quietly changed to a silky smooth ride.

I crossed the mighty Missouri River, over to Chamberlain, the furthest east I would go on my journey. Just for the night, I slipped across from Mountain Time to Central Time. I have come to visit a single institution, nestled on the banks of the Missouri, the Akta Lakota Cultural Centre of St. Joseph's Indian School. And it turned out to be well worth the many extra miles. It is a rich repository of Lakota artifacts, beautifully presented. At the back, on the banks of the river, is a giant Medicine Wheel garden, decorated with sacred and healing herbs and plants with lucid explanations of the multi-layered meaning of each quadrant and color. The quality of the Centre and the campus attest not only to its multi-million dollar financial resources but also to how thoughtfully and effectively it is being spent. The eye-watering prices at its excellent gift shop provide further testimony to its finances. Waaaaay out of my league, I mourn, eyeing several items wistfully.

Chamberlain is a laid-back town with little to commend special attention, except its commanding riverine location. The parking lot of my riverbank Best Western had more boats on trailers than cars. I picked up a few more interesting road signs on the way. There was "Bad River" – though I never figured why it had been naughty. The advertisement for a local restaurant earned a chuckle, "Mexican food so good that President Trump will want to put a wall around it."

Clockwise from top: Reunion of Native veterans of the Battle of the Little Bighorn; decommissioned nuclear missile silo, South Dakota; once the terror of the Cold War, now terrorized by cows; beautifully recreated 1880s Town at Murdo; original Wells Fargo stagecoach at 1880s Town.

Clockwise from top left: Rapid City's tribute to the differently abled; original signage from Checkpoint Charlie, at the Berlin Wall Memorial in Rapid City; sacred Bear Butte, the heart of everything that is; ol' faithful 'Dak'; Vernell White Thunder.

DAY 17: 6 JUNE - BACK TO THE FUTURE

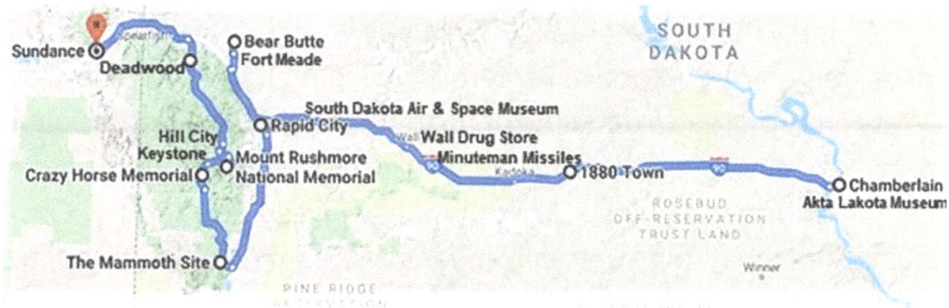

Today I have been time-traveling, much like the celluloid Doc Brown. Like in the movie, "Back to the Future," I feel my car has zipped into a time-machine mode, sliding between the past, present, and future. An overcast sky gave me hope of rain, to save me the hassle of having to run my weary car through a wash. It was not to be, so I pressed on, dust, dirt and all. There is a joy in being filthy that only the lazy know!

As I re-crossed the Missouri, heading west onto the high plains, I slipped back not just into the Mountain time zone (switching time zones twice in two days within the same State is a bit disorienting), but all the way to 1880 – to the delightful 1880s Town just off the I-90 near Murdo. A sign at the entrance claims, "Population: 170 ghosts, 9 cats, 3 dogs, and 3905 rabbits." I guess the number of rabbits keeps changing hourly!

This fascinating recreation is a collection of authentic period buildings crammed to their rafters with artifacts, most genuine, with a few painstakingly crafted reproductions, all artfully weathered and presented with a careful, aging layer of dust. These include soldiers' boots and old Army saddlebags from the Battle of the Little Bighorn, and a saloon piano from Deadwood in its heyday. At various points, sound effects add to the atmosphere. In this milieu are many items from the sets of "Dances with Wolves" and other films. On one wall, a historic black-and-white photograph records a September 1948 reunion of a group of 8 Native warriors, veterans of the Little Bighorn battle. It even boasts a diner inside a real Santa Fe Railroad coach. Of course, being middle America, it could not resist a dollop of kitsch! It was a most enjoyable voyage into the past.

Mentally making poor jokes my family would have cringed at – a roadside sign read "Food exits here," whereas I had always thought it exits elsewhere – takes some of the monotony out of long, straight freeways, through endless grazing fields, stretching out to every horizon with not a living soul for what feels like an eternity. Once again, I see what 'big sky' really means. When you look around, for what seems like hundreds of miles in every direction, and see not a single living thing nor geographic feature or man-made structure of any sort, or even a solitary tree, you have the queasy feeling of being the last person alive in the entire universe, lonely under a giant sky.

Flashing from the past to the future, from the 1880s Town to the Minuteman Missiles site, I made the mistake of ignoring my originally planned route and instead, succumbed to the siren song of my disembodied Garmin lady. Consequently, instead of riding the smooth I-90, I ended up on the barely graded Cottonwood Road, supposedly a backwoods short-cut. However, by this time, even the Garmin lady had been rattled into apparent insanity as she suddenly instructed me, in the middle of nowhere, to turn right – bang into a stout, barbed-wire fence, exactly opposite the direction I needed to go! After much head-scratching good, old-fashioned paper maps, and intuition, came to my rescue. Eventually, I rounded a corner, to face a most incongruous 20th Century sight. Amidst those endless empty vistas, surrounded by herds of peacefully grazing Herefords, hunkers the deadly menace of an underground nuclear missile silo.

At the height of the Cold War over 1000 Minuteman nuclear missiles hid in plain sight, under the prairie grass of these Great

Plains. At this site alone, 15 launch control facilities controlled 150 Inter-Continental Ballistic Missiles, their sinister, doomsday snouts aimed at distant devastation. Superimposing Armageddon on this bucolic scene is mind-bending. Decommissioned in the 1990s, a few of the silos and command centers have become tourist attractions. At the Visitor Centre near the Delta-01 Control Facility, the openness and honesty with which the displays explain the various accidents at the country's nuclear facilities, and near misses that could have destroyed significant parts of the world, struck me powerfully. The meaning of "mutually assured destruction" is amply clear.

A 20-minute drive from the Control Facility is the Delta-9 missile silo. Braving more snake warnings, I walked out to this modern-day Godzilla and peered down into the silo, at that still-chilling, end-of-the-world missile, crouched underground with silent menace. It gave me the shivers - especially when I recall that today's world appears to be heading into another Cold War, or worse. It is sobering to realize that these missiles may be decommissioned but others, even deadlier, are still live, dotted around the country, poised to deliver instantaneous oblivion.

Moving away, my time-machine does another flip, and takes me back to 1890, in search of the privately-funded Wounded Knee Museum at Wall, somewhere off the I-90. Not only are they reputed to have extensive photographs and other items of the massacre, but they also run an ongoing campaign to petition Congress to rescind the reprehensible Medals of Honor awarded for it. Another of their campaigns is attempting to convince sports teams to stop misappropriating Native names and symbols. I would love to sign up to support both petitions. Unfortunately, the Museum appears to have moved. Not easily deterred, after many inquiries and several wrong turns, I track it down to its new location – only to find it closed indefinitely because of a family emergency. Much disappointed, I store it away in my mind for a future trip – hopefully.

Abruptly, I am shot back to the present as I stop for lunch at the very modern-day, ultimate heaven of kitsch, the famous Wall Drug Store. For aficionados of this cultural ethos, it is probably akin to entering the Pearly Gates! A massive, rambling edifice taking up a full city block, it is impossible to work out whether it is one giant store, or a rash of mushrooming, independent stores. Chockfull of kitschy merchandise, entertainment and food outlets, it is a massive visual and sensory overload. I had to sit down, giant hotdog in hand, to take it all in. "Wowzer!" I overheard a Midwesterner exclaim breathlessly. Wowzer, indeed!

I head back onto good old I-90 and notice that it is now littered with huge billboards on various Christian themes, especially anti-abortion. One, in particular, screams repeatedly, "It's a Child, not a Choice." This is, evidently, the Bible belt.

A final, brief stop at the South Dakota Air & Space Centre at Ellsworth Air Force Base near Box Elder, provides me an opportunity to eyeball, up close and personal, the biggest aircraft of different eras. But above all, there, in the heart of South Dakota, in the land of the Dakota folk, sits a beautiful, beautiful Dakota DC-3 aircraft in all her glory, triggering a tsunami of nostalgic memories from my Assam tea estate childhood. It seems only yesterday that my little sister and I were being lifted to the bottom step of the aluminum boarding ladder (and a short, vertical ladder is exactly what it was), its bottom rung several feet off the ground, and helped up the steep ascent inside, scrambling over tea chests lining the upward sloping aisle to our seats – and our barf bags! We would have been heading home from boarding school for the three-month winter holiday. The landing strip, near our home on the tea estate, was just a roughly mown patch of grass and, as the heavy 'Dak' lumbered ponderously into its landing approach, fighter jets from the nearby Indian Air Force station would gleefully buzz it from all directions in teasing good humor that the long-suffering 'Dak' pilots were well used to, every week. On the ground, when it was time for it to take off again, everyone at the airstrip pitched in to push its tail around with sheer muscle-power so it faced the right direction, into the wind. Those were the days, my friend. This aircraft once flew the highly dangerous Hump, the route from Calcutta in India, over the

Himalayas, transporting essential supplies to China during World War II. Very few survived to tell that tale. This beauty did.

Time flows quietly but inexorably on. A rollercoaster day slowly fades into the gloaming, as I roll quietly into Rapid City. Tourist literature informs me it has just 70,000 residents (about the population of a small village in India), receives more sunshine than Miami or Honolulu (which I still find difficult to believe), and is just 60 miles southeast of the geographic centre of the country at Belle Fourche (I never figured out how that might be). My America's Best Value Motel does look to be good value, with spacious, clean and – surprise! surprise! – pleasant-smelling rooms. However, I am now tired of my itchy, new-look beard. Maybe its days are numbered. If so, my wife, at least, will be pleased!

DAY 18: 7 JUNE - THE BERLIN WALL ... IN SOUTH DAKOTA?

Over my leisurely Motel breakfast, I lazily observed my fellow travelers and mused idly on stereotypes. Despite Rapid City being ranked the third most racist city in America, most white folk here, I found, will greet you. Men are usually in shorts and women, puzzlingly, in what appears to be sleeping pajamas, discussing plans to visit the "theai-ter". The men are usually silent and contemplative. African Americans ignore you but are quick to apologize if they feel they have somehow got in your way, even if they have not really. They are almost all women in track-suited groups. To Indians (the ones from, or recently migrated from, India), fellow Indians are transparent, and they will go to great lengths not to see you, under any circumstances. If forced to take notice of you, they will look at you like a faintly disgusting alien lifeform under a microscope. Finally, the Chinese, always aggressive, glare at you like you stole their children.

During my researches I had come across an interesting concept, Rollin Rez Arts, a mobile arts support facility that toured around the Reservations, bringing supplies and succor to artists in its remote, far-flung reaches and conveying their art to galleries in Rapid City. It seemed such a brilliant innovation, I was keen to talk to its organizers, the First Peoples Fund, based right here in Rapid City. To my disappointment, my several emails elicited no response from the person responsible for it and seemed to confirm that it is defunct, as someone had told me at the Oglala Lakota College, on whose grounds I saw the bus forlornly parked. What a huge pity for such an interesting innovation to wither. Still, I would have loved to talk to the people behind it – apparently, the feeling was not reciprocated, as I could get no response out of them.

With dimming hope, I phoned the Wounded Knee Museum in Wall to check if they were now open again. I would have happily made the 100-mile round trip just to see it, as it sounded so promising. They were still closed. The family emergency must be a serious one.

Finally, sallying forth into the city, I am reminded a little of San Rafael in Marin County, California. Other than an eyesore of a big, ugly Dakota Mill & Grain plant in the heart of town, the "City of Rapid City" is a small, relaxed, pretty place. Traffic is very light. I park for free on the campus of the much-anticipated Journey Museum but, again, save that visit for later, like a hoarded treat.

Just down the road, I stroll through the lovely little Memorial Park with its small pond and mini Geneva-style jet d'eau, with picturesque Rapid Creek, the one on whose banks the great Crazy Horse was born, flowing rapidly through it, like it is late for an important meeting. A wonderful place for walkers and cyclists, I can easily visualize whole families spending hours enjoying it. But I have miles to go and places to see, so I scurry along Main Street to a quiet corner of the Park that houses its Berlin Wall Memorial. This contains two authentic sections of the original Berlin Wall and a sign and tank-trap from Checkpoint Charlie. Puzzled about a Berlin Wall memorial in Rapid City, of all places, I hunted down a marker that explained it. Potsdam is a sister city of Sioux Falls. This, I thought, was quite a stretch as Potsdam is not Berlin and Sioux Falls is not Rapid City! Ah, well...it looks pretty anyway, and preserves a piece of history, so, I guess, just let them have their Memorial, however much of a stretch the link may be.

As I stood contemplating such unfathomable mysteries, the adorable little City View Trolley stopped right in front of me, and so I hopped on, to gain something of an overview of the city. Though a pleasant ride, even the Trolley could not find enough in Rapid City to take up more than an hour. The presumably fascinating commentary onboard was drowned out by two old ladies from "Minne-sodah" gossiping right across the length of the Trolley at the top of their voices, without the slightest care for others who may have a little less interest in the engrossing details of their seemingly utterly dreary, scandal-free daily lives. At the top of the tour, the Trolley called at the exquisite little wooden Chapel on the Hill, an authentic piece of Norway right here in South Dakota. If I did not have the unbearable temptation of the Journey Museum gnawing at me, I would have happily hopped off to spend an hour reveling in its tranquil solitude. This serenity in the bosom of Nature, I thought, is what all places of contemplation should be about.

Touting itself as the City of the Presidents, Rapid City has a statue, and a street named for each American President, from the time the dinosaurs roamed the earth right up to the current President, Donald Trump. The only President missing, on any literature, street name, or pedestal, is the country's only African American leader.

After a rapid lunch on Main Street, it was finally time for the lollipop – The Journey Museum I had so looked forward to seeing all these months. It proved to be a remarkable place; worth every bit of the hype I had read about it – a true lollipop.

Most un-Museum-like, it encourages visitors, especially children, to touch and experience its exhibits. There is hardly anything with the usual stern "Do not touch" prohibition. Not only are their collections awesome but, to my considerable surprise in this allegedly racist city, I found their narrative of the Native American experience fair and nuanced. Of course, every museum I have visited so far displays the inexplicable American obsession with guns. The Journey Museum is no exception.

DAY 19: 8 JUNE - BEHOLD, THE HOLY MOUNTAIN

It was frightening! Vernell White Thunder and I were on our way to Bear Butte, the most sacred mountain of the Lakota and other Native Nations. Chatting along I-90, at just over 80 mph, we were tucked behind a long, double-decker vehicle carrier, when it suddenly wiggled crazily across the lanes in a Chinese dragon dance! A red Toyota, dwarfed alongside it in the next lane, barely escaped being swiped into the roadside ditch by the dragon's tail. Fortunately, the trucker regained control and all ended well, but it was frightening enough for me to ease off on the accelerator and lag, demurely, well behind.

Last night, a hailstorm, with baseball-sized hailstones, barely missed Rapid City. What is it with me and natural phenomenon chasing after me! This morning, the early mist burned away to reveal another exquisite, sunny, and cool morning. With nary a cloud in the sky, there was no hope of a natural car wash today either. The Motel had been good, though bulbs in the room kept fusing with mysterious unexpectedness. More natural phenomena? Contrary to popular folklore, I have found people here friendly. Possibly the bias is openly visible only against Native Americans.

Vernell White Thunder is descended of an old, illustrious line. Originally of the Northern Cheyenne, his oldest known ancestor, according to their oral tradition, was a Medicine Man who was the Keeper of the tribe's most revered Sacred Arrows, stolen from him by their traditional foes, the Pawnee. Akin to the Christians' Holy Grail, these hallowed relics, in a very belated gesture of conciliation, are soon to finally be restored to the Cheyenne by the Pawnee. White Thunder's father, more Lakota than Cheyenne, was a Chief, and Vernell is a rare, fluent Lakota speaker and practitioner of their traditional faith. Not a Medicine Man himself, he is, nevertheless, deeply immersed in Lakota spirituality, values, and practices. I am privileged to have an authority like him show me around Bear Butte.

With my few Lakota words picked up from my readings, he understands I am no dilettante and opens up wholeheartedly. A man of wide interests, White Thunder studied psychology, law, and mining and, at various times, worked all those professions. He has traveled extensively around the world, and now owns the sprawling White Thunder Ranch near Kyle, where he used to run cattle but now only raises horses, in the best Cheyenne tradition. Besides being a Veteran, he was a Rodeo rider at one point in his many-splendored career.

Despite living so actively in the contemporary world, White Thunder is an ardent follower of their traditional customs and traditions. His daughter, who lives on his ranch, follows in his spiritual footsteps. Sadly, for him, his son, who lives in Denver, has no interest in the "old ways."

Since 1978, Native spirituality is no longer banned as criminal activity, but it took years of Dr. Martin Luther King Jr.'s civil rights crusade to achieve it. Till then, egged on primarily by the Jesuits of the late 19th Century, even a suspicion of the practice of the ancient Pipe religion incurred severe punishments, a fine of $10,000 (a crippling sum then) and imprisonment for 10 years. Holy Medicine Men were often quietly immured in the Hiawatha All-Indian Insane Asylum in Canton, South Dakota, and rarely ever seen again. So, the movie "One Flew Over the Cuckoo's Nest" has a factual basis.

He, too, feels that tribal government is dangerously corrupt and ineffective. Unless a strong leader emerges soon, their very existence, already regularly menaced by South Dakota's white legislators, will continue to hang in precarious balance. Over lunch, later in Rapid City, I notice his slight unease and wonder about racism against the Lakota. White Thunder tells me of a study that found Rapid City to be the third most racially prejudiced city in America, after Las Vegas and Denver.

"You can palpably feel it, even in restaurants. It is not against me personally, or even generally against people of color, but specifically against all Native Americans," he explains, "Perhaps it is because of a feeling of inherited guilt, as with modern Germans? It probably is the knowledge of what their ancestors did, and that legally, they are nothing more than encroachers on Native lands. Another factor that worries the whites is the dependence of Rapid City's economy on the substantial monies spent there by the Natives from the Reservations, and that Native Americans own almost 20% of Rapid City."

A little-known nugget, that.

Up ahead of us looms Mato Paha, Bear Butte, the most sacred place of many Native peoples, nestled in one corner of the Black Hills, the place of their origin myths, "the heart of all that is." As we wander reverentially through the – as usual – rattlesnake-ridden prairie grasses up the slopes of the Holy Mountain, I suddenly feel goose-bumps and the hair on my arms stir with a life of their own. Shocked, I glance covertly around but do not see anyone else experiencing it. There is some strange, eerie, mystic force on that mountain, something even I, the ultimate skeptic atheist, can neither explain nor deny. You feel it, like a powerful magnetic field, the moment you step on the mountain, while equally inexplicably, it releases you the moment you are off it. I have absolutely no idea what I just experienced, but that I have experienced something otherworldly is beyond even my doubting. White Thunder smiles gently to himself, understanding my inner turmoil with perfect insight. He is no stranger to the mysteries of this mystic mountain.

Our wanderings brought us to two Lakota, praying fervently in a secluded glade and, to my great surprise, he takes me over. The mandatory buffalo skull lies in front of them, facing east where the sun rises, symbolizing White Buffalo Calf Woman who brought the spiritual rituals to the Lakota, accompanied by feathers and dream-catchers to waft their prayers to the Great Spirit. One of them prayed to Mother Earth, Father Sky and the Four Directions, while his friend supported him by singing holy songs. White Thunder joined in their sacred song (Lakota are expected to always take part, in support, and not just spectate), though I could not. It turned out they were from Washington D.C. and had been praying for several days. It impressed me the whole morning that, despite being a stranger, I was always made welcome by everyone, even amid their sacred rituals, chatted with and offered whatever food and drink they had. And no conversation was complete without the incomparable, dry Native wit!

Many Native Americans, from a variety of tribes all across the country, men and women, young and old, come to sacred Bear Butte to pray, some even undertaking the arduous full Vision Quest. There is an understandable desperate hunger in them for some form of guidance for their life and identity and some have come here more than once, braving the rattlesnakes and the unpredictable elements, to beseech the Great Spirit while, often, their family and friends camp at the base of the mountain to lend moral support. Sadly, there are hardly any holy Medicine Men left to guide and succor them in their aching quest, as is so critically needed. It has left these young people spiritually bereft, to fend for themselves without a mentor, and they are doing so with searing yearning.

Further up the slopes, we meet one of several men and women who have come here to pray, a young Apache visiting with his Lakota friend, excited, nervous and scared, having come to holy Bear Butte for his first Vision Quest, the intense ritual of up to four days of total abstinence from food and water, alone up among the higher crags of the mountain, naked to the elements, utterly focused on singing, and praying, "crying for a vision" to guide one's life, through prayers to Mother Earth, Father Sky and the Four Directions. Capable of inducing a very deep, meditative trance, it sometimes, but not always, offers a brief glimpse of one's future and the "other side." Natives believe time is a continuum, without beginning or end and, through such prayers offered by a pure heart, it is occasionally possible to "see beyond." It requires at least a full year of preparing one's mind and purifying one's soul. The young Apache had no holy man to guide him but undeterred, he had chosen his spot, about halfway up the mountain, and was about to plunge into a two-day, rather than a full four-day, Vision Quest. He said he badly needed direction for his life, "especially these days." Silently soaking in all I hear and see, on that strangest of mountains, something, perhaps long-dormant, stirs within my own soul, as though from a waking dream; the proud skeptic falters.

Most traditional Native Americans are unusually close to Nature and the spiritual world "beyond". It is woven inextricably into the very warp and weft of their everyday lives, embedded so profoundly into daily practices that often they are not even consciously considered. The power and accuracy of these visions are beyond explanation and are so documented, well before the events happen, that they are undeniable. Crazy Horse who, on a rare occasion, addressed the assembled tribes at Teaching Hill, here on Bear Butte, experienced a shiver of prophesy that foretold he would never be touched by soldiers' bullets but would be pulled down by the hands of his own people. Events would unfold exactly as foretold, so many years later. Another great handsome, charismatic Chief, Roman Nose, accurately envisioned he would die at Beecher Island, the very morning of his death, as he had touched food with a metal spoon, contrary to his medicine. Sitting Bull's famous vision of soldiers falling upside down into their camp, on the eve of the Battle of the Little Bighorn, has been extensively documented. Even today, White Thunder confirms, it is far from uncommon for the elderly to have such visions and predict future events, or even the personalities of their children and grandchildren. Many of these have been recorded and verified by the indisputable light of events, years later.

Grandparents play an unusually important role in bringing up children in traditional Lakota families, and their memories and teachings are very deep-rooted. Small wonder then, if this vital cultural link was severed, whether by boarding schools, missionaries, alcohol or familial deaths, it resulted in tremendous psychological trauma and identity fragmentation. The situation has been aggravated, he added with immense sadness, by the corruption in tribal government which has frittered away scarce resources so badly needed for programs to help these children find their roots again. The tremendous current dearth of spiritual leaders among an essentially intensely spiritual people has left them adrift and rudderless. The need for councilors and mentors is dire.

A Dakota we met on Bear Butte told me that there are now just 33 living speakers of their Dakota dialect, while the Assiniboine have only three. The threatened extinction of entire species is not limited to the animal world. The Lakota language, too, has suffered serious threat, as most of their children can no longer speak it, primarily because their parents have forgotten it, had it beaten out of them in boarding schools, or been reduced to alcoholism and substance abuse. Today, as Peter Matthiessen so succinctly puts it, "the new fashion in racism...is to pretend that the real Indians are all gone."

Fortunately, a slow but certain resurgence has begun, and revival is underway. It is now the time of the seventh generation that Crazy Horse predicted.

Deplorably, the desecration of sacred Bear Butte continues apace with the world-famous annual Motorcycle Rally at nearby Sturgis becoming the newest source of irritation and friction for traditional Natives. Despite the area of Bear Butte being strictly protected by Treaty, the motorcycle riders are encroaching more and more each year with complete impunity, most ignorant of the significance of this holy mountain, others not caring. There is even some momentum among local politicians to grab chunks of that land to build biker bars and strip joints, right on the edges of the Natives' most sacred, and last remaining, holy place, to reinforce the economic boost that the Sturgis Motorcycle Rally brings them each year. When I queried White Thunder about this latest venality, this powerful modern warrior's characteristically gentle response was, "We are like fleas on the land – humans can't really own the land. The white man has never understood that."

Wending our way back, we drive briefly through Fort Meade, the place where the Star-Spangled Banner first became music for the Retreat, long before it was to become one of the most unusual national anthems of the world. It was also the place where the shattered 7th Cavalry reformed after the debacle of the Little Bighorn. In 1944, it became a VA Hospital and today, there is very little around to show it was ever a Fort at all, let alone one with any special significance in history. I am unimpressed, and I notice White Thunder has a look of reserve, so we do not tarry.

We head pensively back towards Rapid City. I am silent for once, and White Thunder quietly allows me the mental space. He knows it cannot but have been an intense experience for me. Bear Butte, the Holy Mountain, apparently always is, for the open-hearted. Less than an hour later, I plummet from the spiritual heights to the mundanely material, as the city swallows us. Rapid City is a quaint little place, amidst lush, low hills, full of charming lakes, parks, and woods. It is the only city I have ever visited that has colorful art beautifying even the usually ugly street switchgear, and a monument celebrating the differently-abled. Bravo, City of Rapid City!

Another horde of pernicious vultures that would plague the Native Nations for centuries to come, Christian missionaries accompanied the ruthless land-grab of the past. With a few sterling exceptions, these priests, frequently Jesuits, rode out to save the 'savage' souls of "our Indian wards", bringing the strange invention of the Devil, for blackmail, and a man-like Father in the sky who would forgive even your most heinous sins, as bribery. Few Natives could fathom the concept of a Great Father who cruelly punished the mistakes of his creatures by condemning them to burn in fires for all eternity. As James Wilson puts it in his "The Earth Shall Weep", "...there is almost no Native American equivalent to the Judeo-Christian idea of a kind of communal sin, an inherited curse which isolates us and opposes us to a hostile material world." Their own Great Spirit is a far kinder, gentler, more supportive parent.

As Red Cloud once eloquently said, "When the white man came, he had the Bible and we had the land. Then, we had the Bible, and he had the land."

These were typified by Reverend Samuel Dutton Hinman, who passionately advocated that the Natives should have less land and more Christianity, all the while unobtrusively swindling them out of huge tracts of their best lands for his own personal enrichment. These so-called men of God simply could not wait for rewards in Heaven.

Heading back into Rapid City, I collect a few more interesting street names – "Disk Drive" and "9-11 Road", while "Lame Johnny Creek" had me curious about its backstory. Susceptible to an alternate interpretation was "Windbreak Road." The Firehouse Brewery's billboards all feature an eye-catching real, bright-red fire engine, though I could not make the connection between a fire truck and "South Dakota's finest brewery", beyond the tenuous link of the branding. Back at the motel, it is my laundry day again. As I moodily watch the machine churn, the gradually darkening skies open up with a benediction of rain, like a healing balm. A portent of peace, harmony, and conciliation to come, I wonder?

DAY 20: 9 JUNE - TASUNKO WITKO

This Motel too is, predictably, owned by a Gujarati Patel. It has an attractive facade in a charming Spanish-Mexican style. Custer is a *really* tiny town, just 5 miles from the Crazy Horse Memorial. It is the quintessential one-horse town, though I did not see even the one horse around. Insensitive to the Lakota, Custer town is in Custer State Park, within Custer County. It feels historically uncomfortable for the names of Crazy Horse and Custer to jostle on the same street signs. However, perhaps there is justice because his mammoth mountain memorial will, one day, utterly dominate the Black Hills, sharply diminishing the Custer namesakes scattered about its feet. Mysteriously, a few days before his murder, Crazy Horse had a vision and revealed to his followers that one day he would return – but in stone! Inyan, rock, was always one of his spiritual powers.

Outward bound from Rapid City, I headed first to the Mammoth Site, at Hot Springs. It was another lovely day, with the breath-taking backdrop of the Black Hills gowned in ponderosa pine, startlingly black against the lush green of the plains around. I learned later that ponderosa branches have one side that absorbs light, making them look black. Hence, the Black Hills.

A pleasant, relaxed drive brought me to this amazing place, and I was glad I had included this detour in my plans. A construction contractor had uncovered a treasure-trove of mammoth skeletons and, in a rare, unselfish gesture, handed the site over for preservation. Over 60 mammoth skeletons, curiously all male, litter this small soak-pit, of which just a third have been excavated so far. The experts believe it will take a century to complete uncovering them all and, by then, it could reveal even more. These ancient skeletons put time and human strivings in perspective. Several of these are Columbian mammoths, which were even larger than the better known Woolly Mammoths. Oddly, a few of these Columbian mammoths strayed over to some islands off the Californian coast, during the Ice Age, and eventually evolved into a dwarf mammoth species there, somewhat like baby elephants.

Highway 16A is twisty, narrow, steep, and requires the driver's complete attention. It repays that effort with what has to be one of the world's most scenic routes. There are stunning vistas everywhere, which compelled me to make frequent stops. The half-hour journey took over an hour, thanks to these exquisite distractions. There are several tunnels en route, with a couple that have a quick succession of tunnels within a very short distance, looking rather like a Mammoth ribcage. Stunningly framed views of Mount Rushmore appear through many of them. Fortunately, I was driving up from the south, which direction offers the most dramatic views. Passing motorists were invariably patient and indulgent with my frequent, breathless stops.

This is the land of Tasunko Witko, Crazy Horse (more accurately, His Horses Are Crazy), the Strange Man of the Oglala, probably the greatest Native, or even North American, warrior of all time. The man who never 'touched the pen' to sign any treaty in his life; the man the US Army could never conquer or break in spirit. There is justice in this gigantic mountain being carved to memorialize him (actually, only the likeness of his spirit, since he allowed no one to photograph him), dominating the sacred Black Hills he fought so hard to save for his people. A fitting response to the pettiness that named the surrounds after the man who opened the floodgates to the despoiling of Paha Sapa, Custer.

The scale of this mountain carving is epic, the largest ever attempted by man. Like the Taj Mahal in my native India, it's magnificent, heroic scale cannot be visualized through photographs and has to be viewed in situ to be fully appreciated. All the four Presidents on Mount Rushmore, themselves gargantuan, could easily fit into just a small part of his head, while the big bus I rode to the base of the mountain could comfortably travel through the pupil of his eye! His horse will eventually stand 22 stories tall. Conceived by Chief Henry Standing Bear, he approached Polish-American mountain sculptor, Korczak Ziolkowski in 1939, to execute it. Since the first blasting in 1948, nineteen million tons of rock have been blasted, and they expect the work to take at least another 70 years to complete. After Korczak passed away, his wife, Ruth, completed the face in 1998, and many of their ten children continue the work today. I am glad my children, or their children, will see it finished. The monumental work already attracts 1.5 million visitors, just a shade less than Mount Rushmore does, and perhaps its greatest contribution is in making these millions aware of the Native American side of the story, that they too had heroes as glorious, some even more so, than any on the other side. Deserving to be on everyone's bucket list, the bus ride to the base of the mountain is an experience that cannot be described. For a more significant donation, it is even possible to take a small van right to the top – for the non-vertigo-afflicted, unlike me. It has to be a view well worth vertigo-ing for!

The Black Hills are extraordinarily beautiful, and it is easy to appreciate the Natives' reverence for their Paha Sapa; their horror at its wanton desecration. In 1874, in blatant violation of the Lakota's treaty rights, Lieutenant Colonel Custer led an expedition to 'discover' gold in the Black Hills, and "open it up" to a flood of miners who neither understood nor cared for its significance to the Lakota. One can appreciate, if not condone, the Americans' desperate need for its bountiful gold which undoubtedly saved the country's economy from recession. Gold, worth billions of dollars has, since, flowed out of the Black Hills – the Homestake Mine, alone, extracted over $1.5 billion worth over the years, fully half of US gold production – with not a single dollar's worth, in the 150 years, going to benefit those who, even today, legally own the Hills, the Lakota. Understandably, Custer's route through these Hills came to be known to the Natives as "the thieves' road."

The succinct comment of a contemporary Congressman summed the prevalent mood, "It is ridiculous nonsense to let the Sioux chase buffalo through the Black Hills when there are millions in gold waiting to be mined."

However, Justice Blackmun at the US Supreme Court, in 1980, pulled no punches, stating bluntly, "A more ripe and rank case of dishonorable dealings will never, in all probability, be found in our history."

His judgment though, still did not return the land to its rightful owners, but awarded them financial compensation which, in today's money, is worth about a billion dollars, an award that the Lakota, despite their poverty and desperate financial need, have refused to accept as they cannot ever consider surrendering their most sacred land. It speaks much of the profound significance it holds for them, well beyond anything that can be valued in gold or greenbacks. The grab-it-all attitude of the miners showed through in Custer's response to a reporter.

When asked, "Aren't the Black Hills officially Sioux land from the treaty of 1868?" his response was, "Whatever the right or wrong isn't the question. The Indians must be dispossessed."

Almost all Native lands were appropriated under "Manifest Destiny", "Eminent Domain", "Civilizing the Savage", or similar fantasies but, in truth, it was a blind grab for gold or oil or coal, resources the Natives did not value at all and never objected to the wasicu taking freely, so long as they could keep their buffalo, their lifestyle, their ancient culture, an elemental defense of family, tribe, home, and hearth. Undoubtedly, both could have coexisted peacefully. Why, oh why, could a genuinely great Nation, the land of the free and home of the brave, not find it in its heart to spare the home of the bravest of the brave, or the liberty of those who had always been free?

A half-hour ride out to the base of the mountain, for a nominal charge, turned out to be some of the best money I spent on this trip. Spectacular from afar, the sculpture is overwhelming viewed from its base. The guide laughingly encouraged us to carry away as many authentic chips of the mountain as we wished, from the huge piles lying around. As he explained, tongue firmly in cheek, they need to move thousands of tons of the stuff and would appreciate any help from us! I was keen to watch the nightly laser tribute that happens after dark against the mountainside. Unfortunately, at this time of the year, at this latitude, dusk descends only around 10.30 at night. I was just too tired to wait quite that long. Which compelled me to also give up on my planned Tatanka Stew (bison stew) dinner at their Laughing Water restaurant and instead settle for a delicious buffalo burger for a late lunch. I have never tasted such exquisite meat before, and have to say it is considerably superior to beef, pork, lamb, venison, mutton – perhaps even human!

Before leaving, I took the time to browse through their excellent Indian Museum, Native American Educational & Cultural Center, and the sculptor Korczak Ziolkowski's original home and studio. Crazy Horse's story is told here with simple honesty. Several fascinating artifacts include Sitting Bull's huge bow and arrows. Plans are afoot to create a medical university for Native students on the campus. These were very well spent hours, and I left with the impression that here, at last, an attempt is being made to do justice to this larger-than-life hero. A quote on their walls stayed with me, "When the legends die, the dreams end. When the dreams end, there is no more greatness." Truth distilled.

On my winding way along the often very narrow and steep, but highly picturesque, Highway 16A, I passed Mount Rushmore though I did not stop, expecting long queues to enter. The pull-offs along the road provide equally wonderful views. This breathtaking masterpiece by Borglum fully justifies its fame and is undoubtedly one of the great achievements of mankind. I think I passed more cars on Highways 244 & 385 to Mount Rushmore than I had in the whole of Rapid City.

While it is, understandably, the focus of American patriotism and pride, few understand the Native perspective, and even fewer, it seems, care. Images of the invader chiefs carved out of their sacred Six Grandfathers Hill is akin to placing a monstrous statue of the Devil in the middle of St. Peter's Square at the Vatican. Two of those Presidents owned and traded Native slaves, while the most beloved of them, Abraham Lincoln, was responsible for the largest single hanging in US history, almost a State lynching, when 39 innocent Dakotas were killed to appease the hysteria of white settlers in Mankato, Minnesota. Ironically, they were all recent converts to Christianity who went to the gallows singing a Christian hymn in their language, which the local Press, unable to understand, labeled "heathenish, savage, Indian wailing." Later, the founder of the famous Mayo Clinic took away the bodies, for experimentation to see if they were human. These brave patriots had fought the settlers not for some abstract ideal like conquering territory, but for the simple need to protect their families. They had not invaded a foreign land, to snatch something not theirs; they had simply tried to defend home, hearth, family and people. However, change had come, and it was irreversible.

Clockwise from top left: Crazy Horse memorial, being sculpted in the Black Hills of South Dakota; at the foot of the mountain being sculpted for the Crazy Horse memorial; Mount Rushmore drive-by; the beautiful Black Hills; 1880s Train chugging slowly through the Black Hills; stunning Highway 16A.

Clockwise from top left: Original invitation to the UN to set up its headquarters in the Black Hills; original poster for Buffalo Bill's Wild West Show; tepee on the lovely Pine Ridge Reservation; apt warning in Deadwood; site of first gold find in Deadwood.

DAY 21: 10 JUNE - CHOO CHOO TRAIN

I have now been on the road for three weeks, and the fatigue seeping into my ancient bones admonishes me I should have been home yesterday! Yet, the irresistible siren-song of the open road still has me in its thrall. I am happy to have this relaxed day, enjoying the beautiful Black Hills, away from the searing ache of the Native American experience, and the exuberant derring-do of the frontiersmen, the indomitable free spirits who built this great country. I write in my notebook as I chug drowsily along on an excruciatingly cute little 1880s train out of Keystone, heading for lunch at Hill City, an hour away. After lunch, I shall meander dreamily back to Keystone. Both tiny towns, lost in the folds of the Black Hills, survive only for tourists, evaporating like a mirage come winter.

I arrive at Keystone much too early to check-in. This gives me time to muse on some idiosyncrasies of this wonderful country. For instance, I discovered that each road has its own song. Yes, the roads do sing! I had never noticed before that the sound made by the car's tires is different on changing surfaces, and almost every road seems to have a slightly different surface. The duet of tire and tarmac varies on every road. Then, there is the peculiar devaluation of words and their true worth. Everyone is always "so exciiited" because just about everything is "awesome." You are thanked profusely for even the most mundane inquiry about another, while every person in the military is a "hero," even if he is the most corrupt supply clerk. It is a challenge to differentiate sincerity from superficiality.

It was surprisingly warm in the Black Hills. The short drive from Custer to Keystone is gorgeous. Lovely little lakes pop up, to delight the eye. I stopped at an especially lovely one to stretch my legs, and try my skills at 'art' photography. It was the usual scintillating disaster. Not to mention those contortions almost landed me in the lake, camera and all. While everything in little Custer was within easy strolling distance, Keystone turned out to be even tinier, and everything was, I guess, within sneezing distance. The only difference is that Keystone is on a slope and so, walking up and down its single road reminded me I am a total stranger to gyms. Helicopter tours are popular here and, at any moment, several buzz around, like nosey mosquitoes.

Looked around at the full passenger load, I was glad I had bought my ticket online, months in advance, while still in Oman. It would have been impossible to get one on the day. As the century-old, wooden coaches dash along at a blinding 20 miles per hour to cover the 20 miles from Keystone to Hill City, I reminiscence about the Toy Train of my native Darjeeling in India which, too, a brisk walker could outpace, perhaps even with a nap or two along the way. Each ancient coach has a name and a long history, a far cry from the anonymous steel boxes of modern rolling stock. Inexplicably, some days the trains move under steam and on others diesel. Today, disappointingly, was a diesel day. The staff, in period railroad uniforms, make a special effort to entertain the children aboard. A young girl, also in period costume, moves down the aisle selling popcorn and snacks. The gentle clickety-clack of the wheels is tremendously somniferous, and I have to fight a vigorous battle to keep my eyes from downing shutters.

Fortunately, oblivious to the other passengers' desire to listen to the narrative over the train's PA system, a young father keeps me awake by loudly asking his little son, "So, buddy, are ya havin a good taaaahm?" Buddy, priorities crystal clear, focuses intently on his ice-cream. Grandma ignores the No Smoking signs and puffs away contentedly – till she sees the Conductor approaching, at which point she deftly flicks it out of the open window with practiced nonchalance. Her "lil' ol' granny" expression does not slip for a second. It turns out, this train too is full of 'Minne-sodahs.' That State must be empty in summer.

This 20-mile stretch is the only surviving section of the original Deadwood railroad, which flourished for exactly a hundred years. Near Keystone, we pass the Holy Terror Mine, named after the owner's wife. Halfway along is "Oblivion" while, nearing Hill City, the train passes "Tin Mill Hill." The last few miles of track are steep, and sometimes the locomotive seems to have second thoughts about whether it is worth the struggle. Ambling along among the fragrant Ponderosa pine forests and black granite rocks, the train eventually sighs wearily into Hill City. This hamlet seems to be even smaller than Keystone if that were possible. Lunch, at the largely open-air station is a simple but tasty buffalo burger with "all the fixins," which, of course, in American, means steep mountains of accompaniments! The size of that burger and its 'fixins,' combined with the utter serendipity of the shade-dappled little station in the middle of the hills, sinfully tempted me away from the South Dakota Railway Museum next door and onto a comfortable train-side reclining chair, similar to those that used to grace old train station retiring rooms in colonial India, in the bad old days. A man needs to digest his lunch in peace. Zzzzzz...

I had come out to Hill City in the Edward Gillette closed coach (with open windows) and, in consideration of my ancient bottom, padded seats. These seats could swivel so that a group of four could sit facing each other, a nifty feature. The commentary was humorous and entertaining. The popcorn concessionaire, the young girl who looked like a child herself, came through again and I decided no American journey is complete without popcorn. On the return trip, I chose the wooden seats of the open-sided Redfern coach. At one time, it was a baggage car and seemed to be even more fun than the Edward Gillette. As usual, I was the only Injun in a train-full of cowboys, except for – finally! – one genuine Injun family, enjoying the ride through their own ancient mountains.

Back at Keystone, I strolled languidly along the single street of this Lilliputian town (village?), browsing a few of the shops, much like a cow casually cropping the odd passing bush. One, Dakota Leathers, offered genuine leather bags and luggage at stunningly attractive prices. I picked up a lovely, Native-designed (but made in Mexico) fringed, leather purse for my new daughter-in-law. It left me wishing the owner would sell online and ship internationally!

DAY 22: 11 JUNE - SIN AND DEBAUCHERY

Dawn was a cold 9 Celsius. The Super8 Motel at Keystone was a pleasant enough place. It sat along a sloping hillside and, as a result, looks bizarrely like a building that has buckled in an earthquake. It is a surreal visual effect. At the Reception desk is a, by now, familiar sign. The more I wander around this country, the more astounded I am at tourist destinations with signs advising visitors on the firearms that can be carried in, either concealed or in full public view! Only in America!

The road from Keystone is well signed and every scenic lookout has a pull-off for visitors. I soon learned that, if there is a pull-out, there is scenery worth stopping for. Incongruously, along the way, I passed several large billboards advertising "Red Ass Rhubarb." Fair warning, I guess! A little further along, I can see Black Elk Peak, the highest point between the Rockies and the Alps in Europe. Earlier it was Harney Peak, named for the General even the East Coast newspapers labeled "Squaw Killer Harney," after he infamously butchered Little Thunder's defenseless Cheyenne peace camp on the Blue Water. William Selby Harney was also known to have beaten a defenseless female slave to death. It is some small restitution that it has now been renamed to honor the great Lakota seer, Black Elk.

With considerable amusement, I eye the hordes of bikers on the road. They are mostly elderly, with grey-haired ponytails behind red bandanas, thoroughly confused between the hippie and the Hell's Angel look. Riding pillion is usually a redoubtable female wrestler. In their desperate effort to look formidable and cool, they have forgotten the Haight-Ashbury era is long over.

Eventually, I sidle nervously into a Town of Sin and Debauchery. The leisurely 45-minute drive through the breathless beauty of the mystical Black Hills brings me to, once again, the flip side of the Frontier experience. At Deadwood, I am staying at the famous Historic Franklin Hotel, where rooms near mine have rested John Wayne, Wild Bill Hickok, Theodore Roosevelt, William Taft, Buffalo Bill Cody, and many another celebrity. I feel almost a celebrity myself, in the company of such illustrious ghosts.

If ever there was a town whose foundations are proudly built on unadulterated, unabashed greed and venality, it is Deadwood. A hugely atmospheric town, still thriving on at least one of its hereditary sins, gambling, it was once the heart of the Black Hills gold rush. Deadwood has seen it all. Even in its modern-day determination to push tourism, the only sin from its past it appears not to have revived is prostitution. The gritty, eponymous HBO series had prepared me for the rawness of this once no-holds-barred, lawless and illegal 'camp' on land guaranteed "in perpetuity" to the Lakota by the Treaty of Laramie. In 1877, Al Swearengen operated his bordello, the Gem Theatre, down the road (today the Mineral Palace Hotel, after the original burnt to the ground in one of the several fires to devastate Deadwood over the years), a refuge for gamblers, cardsharps, and, in the exquisite parlance of the day, "soiled doves." In good Deadwood tradition, he met his end in a Denver ditch in 1904, apparently beaten to death, having quit Deadwood in 1899. Nearby was the equally notorious Bella Union Saloon. 11 of every 16 women in Deadwood were 'soiled doves'. The section of Main Street between present-day Wall Street and Highway 85 was the Badlands, so-called as it was the tacitly agreed area outside the jurisdiction of the law, the home of all that was debauched and degenerate – and also home to Deadwood's justifiably notorious Chinatown.

Further down Main Street, witness to so much, past the Northern Hills Model Railroad, is the infamous Saloon No.10 where a cowardly Jack McCall shot the legendary Wild Bill Hickok in the back as he sat playing cards, holding what has come to be known as the Dead Man's Hand. It was the only time in his life that Wild Bill could not sit with his back to a wall and it proved fatal. This street has known not only James Butler "Wild Bill" Hickok, but also Martha "Calamity Jane" Canary, allegedly Wild Bill's girlfriend, celebrated Sheriff Seth Bullock and his wife Martha, the sleazy E.B. Farnum, Wild Bill's close friend Charlie Utter, Bullock's friend and business partner Sol Star, Samuel Fields, the colourful Wong Lee, and the hugely popular Kitty Leroy, all larger-than-life Wild West characters in their own right. Though Calamity Jane died in 1903 in the nearby town of Terry, she was sentimentally brought back and interred near Wild Bill on Mount Moriah. They all now sleep together in the Mount Moriah Cemetery. Deadwood would not be Deadwood if this famous cemetery was not also home to the graves of its celebrated brothel Madams, such as Madame Moustache. Originally in the more gentrified area of Ingleside, they shifted the graves to Mount Moriah in 1878 when that area started developing into a 'respectable' neighborhood. However, it seems they overlooked a few bodies, and there are reports of them showing up at Ingleside construction sites as late as 2012.

The entire town was built on alcohol, prostitution, and opium, riding the heady crest of the gold rush. The law was a rough-and-ready thing at best, and its enforcement both sporadic and hazardous. Guns, grit and, above all, gold built Deadwood. The Homestake Gold Mine finally shut in 2002 after 126 years of operation. The last brothel downed its less-than-discreet shutters as recently as 1980.

Founded in 1874 as a gold rush camp, Deadwood was a tough little gulch and its residents even tougher. A devastating fire destroyed the town in 1879, but it rapidly rebuilt and rose again, phoenix-like. Seth Bullock and Sol Star's shop was one of the victims of that particular fire, but they reincarnated the site into the Bullock Hotel, still operating today – complete with nightly tours to meet Bullock's ghost. Even in a town full of colorful characters, the Canadian, Seth Bullock, stood out. Elected to the Montana Senate when he was barely old enough to vote, he helped pass the resolution, in 1872, which protected the Yellowstone National Park. Later, he was a Captain fighting the Spanish-American War and became a close, lifelong friend of Theodore Roosevelt. It is said, he tamed Deadwood more through strength of character than force.

Almost Divine retribution for its sins, fire and flood destroyed Deadwood several times, over the years, the last in 1959. But Deadwood is still here and prospering. Today, it is no longer the town of sin, greed, and lawlessness, but it uses it's highly picturesque past to good effect to promote tourism, as a baby Las Vegas but with real history and personality. There are regular 'shoot-outs' up and down Main Street, and the assassination of Wild Bill Hickok re-enacted, along with the first, sham trial of Jack McCall. In death, Wild Bill appears to be contributing more to Deadwood's economy than he ever did in life. Even Kevin Costner has got in on the action, probably inspired by his film, "Dances with Wolves", buying up the Midnight Star Casino and a namesake tour company whose excellent one-hour Original Deadwood Tour offers a comprehensive, very humorous overview of the city of sin, thanks to its friendly and funny guide, Dave. It also takes one up to Mount Moriah Cemetery, the final resting place of so many illustrious folk of yesteryear. As it is a fairly steep climb, especially for my somewhat ancient, creaking shanks, I was more than glad to take advantage of Mr. Costner's automotive assistance.

A little outside the Deadwood gulch, Costner has a buffalo ranch where the story of the bison is narrated. Once well over 60 million strong, they are now reduced to less than one thousand, after teetering on the edge of total extinction for decades. Fortunately, modern conservation efforts are slowly bringing them back to the Great Plains, undoing the scorched earth ravages of a soulless Army General a century and a half ago. The descendants of the very last surviving herd from that time now roam a corner of the Golden Gate Park in San Francisco.

I went the whole hog with the tourist thing and picked up a Pastport, the city's tourism promotion scheme for their major attractions. Its biggest attraction, for me, was the offer of unlimited free trolley rides around town and, even more, the chance to win a holiday in the Black Hills. Though, with my usual run of luck, I knew I would, most likely, win a handkerchief to wipe my tears with, as I watched others jet off to that holiday. However, when I did eventually return to the old Railroad Station, now the Visitor Centre, with my Pastport bearing impressive stamps from six attractions, I received a set of nifty Deadwood playing cards in a 'period' tin box. Much better than a handkerchief! Deadwood's clever and enthusiastic tourism promotion efforts, aimed primarily at children, offer several free street shows throughout the day, free or nearly free trolley rides, and a genuinely warm welcome everywhere. The town itself is easily walkable, with little traffic.

As the day was waning, I rode out to the farthest attraction on the trolley, the Days of 76 Museum and the nearby Rodeo Stadium. The present Deadwood Trolley was established in 1992 but is the successor to the Deadwood Street Railroad set up in 1888. On the way, as part of his commentary, the Trolley Driver pointed out the Comfort Inn which he said, is "the only one not Pakistani owned." It seems, like gold, a persistent, thinly-veiled seam of racism does still runs just under the surface. However, most trolley drivers were friendly and chatty. After all, Deadwood takes fun very seriously.

The Museum is largely a storehouse for a variety of coaches from that era. As I wandered among them, I marveled at the sturdy backsides of the men and women of that time, jolting along on nearly non-existent suspensions over rough, rutted, unpaved tracks for hundreds of miles. Even the thought of it makes my posterior ache. They were nothing if not hardy and determined. No doubt, the smell of gold, even gold on illegally occupied land, helped with the determination. Later that evening, I would take a short ride in an authentic Wells Fargo stagecoach, with its very basic single, thin leaf-spring suspension, ambling unhurriedly through the well-paved streets of Deadwood for the benefit of tourists, which confirmed me in my respect for the old settlers' rears!

Between the Museum and the Rodeo stadium, stands the statue of a grizzled old gold miner holding a nugget up to the sun, marking one spot where gold was first discovered in Deadwood. The Rodeo stadium lay asleep, dreaming of the wild whoops and careering hoofs of competitions past.

It was laundry day again but, strangely, I could not locate a single laundry in Deadwood, the place whose Chinatown, in its deadly Badlands, used to be chockfull of laundries, at least officially, though most were, in reality, opium dens, whorehouses, and places to quietly feed dead bodies to the pigs. At my Hotel, after some head-scratching, the Receptionist suggested I might just be able to find one in Lead, a small town about 5 miles down the freeway. Even my well-known Hotel did not offer laundry services. Remarkable!

DAY 23: 12 JUNE - WITNESS TO MURDER

Yet another cold 9 Celsius sunrise streaked my hotel window. At 8.30 am, the entire town was still fast asleep with not even a stray cat stirring anywhere. This is not a morning town. Breakfast was available only at my Hotel, as every cafe and restaurant was still shuttered, deep in dreamland. A lone ice-cream parlor, though, was open for business on this crisp, cold morning! One of the curious things about Deadwood is that it boasts many, many bars, but a strictly limited number of places to eat. Its priorities are abundantly clear. However, true to American tradition which I was very familiar with by now, my breakfast omelet at the Hotel was so gigantic that, later in the day, I could fit in just an ice-cream for lunch, wondering if I could eat anything at all even at dinner. The American appetite is a magnificent beast. After breakfast, I ruminated awhile on a public bench on historic Main Street, enjoying the tepid sunshine and the fast, free wi-fi available everywhere. Idly, I watched old ladies charging the shops with gusto, bags full of kitsch hanging on their walkers. The market is full of Donald Trump memorabilia, reminding me that this is a "managed enfranchisement" State.

Glancing at my fingers, I noticed my nails needed clipping. As I could not carry a pair of nail clipping scissors because of airline restrictions, I set out in search of a shop to buy one. After an hour of futile hunting, I gave up as, evidently, there is not a single retailer in Deadwood selling nail scissors! Folks kindly suggested I buy a drink instead. I would have to continue with witches' fingernails a while longer.

Deliberating further on things Americana, I wondered why there seems to be such a concerted effort to do things differently from the rest of the world. For instance, doors open outwards towards those entering; light switches flip upwards to the 'on' position; the word "small" does not exist at all, while "medium" means gargantuan; a trolley is usually a bus. Hmmm...

My Hotel may be historic, since all those old geezers once stayed there, but its facilities also appear to have been maintained a century ago. The water mixer in the basin mixed only grudgingly; the tired, cracked bathtub sighed with age, ashamed to reveal its chipped enamel; the shower nurtured a decidedly don't-bother-me attitude; the dim lighting may have been 'period' but made reading impossible. Like me, I felt certain the celebrity ghosts would have killed for a coffee machine. After all that 'historic' build-up, the entire effect is rather spoiled by the decidedly un-historic slot machines crammed into every nook and cranny of the ground floor reception and entryway.

A curious historic nugget I picked up was that, despite the Black Hills being stolen by the white settlers, in 1927 Chief Standing Bear inducted President Calvin Coolidge into the Oglala Lakota tribe, with the name Wanbli Tokahe, Leading Eagle. I did not see any sign that he or his successors reciprocated that warm gesture, then or now.

The Adams Museum is chockfull of fascinating exhibits from Deadwood's past. The millionaire Adams bequest of the Museum was conditional on visitors' entry always remaining free of cost. So, today's innovative Museum administrators are trying a workaround by "suggesting" a donation of $5. It seems ethically slightly iffy, though probably financially pragmatic.

At the Adams House Museum, on the contrary, I could not visit on my own, being told that they had scheduled the next tour after several hours. Since I did not see a crowd beating down their door, I skipped it and instead visited a nearby Gold Mine.

The now-defunct, little Broken Boot Goldmine provided a glimpse of Deadwood's raison d'etre. The cheesy jokes of the jaded tour guide, as we wended our way through the mine, matched some signs on the low-roofed, slightly claustrophobic tunnels, "Watch your head, or watch your language!" Besides some old mining equipment lying around, there were several visible veins of different minerals, which the guide pointed out. Unfortunately, not one was of the only metal that matters here!

After my ice-cream lunch, I strolled down nostalgia lane, also known as Main Street. First up, I passed the original Saloon No.10, now the Wild Bill Bar & Trading Post. Though this is where Wild Bill Hickok was really shot, to my puzzlement, another bar down the road is now called Saloon No.10 and hosts a re-enactment of that doleful event. Meanwhile, the original bar is trying desperately to cash in too by charging people to see the spot where it really happened. The chair he was sitting on at the time is on display above the door. Seemingly, anything to do with that shooting results in cash tills jingling here.

Between these two uneasy neighboring bars, across the way from the old Bullock Hotel, sits the Celebrity Hotel, stuffed with curious, Vegas-like memorabilia. The original Herbie, the Volkswagen Beetle of celluloid fame, preens in splendor in its corner, while a showcase on a prominent wall contains Elvis Presley's unmistakable white suit. A wall full of wild and wonderful electric guitars once belonged to an entire pantheon of rock and pop stars, including Metallica, Guns n Roses, Garth Brooks, Charlie Pride, Police, Sheryl Crow, Wynonna Judd, Phil Collins, and Kurt Cobain. I take photographs for my Sons, whose gods some of them are.

A few doors down is Woody's Old Time Wild West Photos, where tourists from the Mid-West are indulging their fantasies by dressing up to be photographed as one (or several) of a spectrum of exotic Wild West characters and stereotypes. It is a well-loved magnet for kids and identity-conflicted adults with mid-life crises. I spent a few minutes watching what must be every psychoanalyst's wet dream, though it did not tempt me.

Shootouts happen to a strict schedule, progressing gradually down Main Street. The Calamity Jane show starts the ball rolling at 1.45 pm (repeated in front of the Franklin, before its shootout), though it is the Tin Lizzie (near the Mineral Palace) that kicks off the first shootout at 2 pm, followed by the Celebrity Hotel a couple of hours later, culminating in a grand finale in front of my Franklin Hotel at 6 pm. The shootouts, despite lacking even the semblance of an attempt at realism, do not get old even with repeated watching.

As the evening shades drew on, I strolled back to my Historic Silverado Franklin Hotel, close to where gold was first struck in Deadwood Gulch. Relaxing over a much-needed cup of caffeine, a flurry of gunshots jolted me. Realizing it was the evening shootout, I hurried across the street to the Masonic Lodge, just in time to watch the trial of Jack McCall. Having witnessed the murder of Wild Bill Hickok at Saloon No.10 earlier, I was keen to see its conclusion.

The only ticketed event of the day's many historic entertainments, it is staged with verve, skill, and humor. Audience members are often hauled up onto the stage to take part as witnesses to the dastardly act, and I suddenly found myself so 'volunteered', despite having studiously avoided eye contact with the 'recruiter,' Andy "Cookie" Mosher, who is Court Clerk now, was gunslinger earlier, and will be stagecoach hand tomorrow! I would get to know the genial, warm Irishman better tomorrow on the Wells Fargo stagecoach but, at that moment, I did not entertain benevolent thoughts about him!

Potbelly wobbling, he laughed warmly at the audience, "It's no use staring at your shoes, to avoid me. I *will* get you!"

And he did.

Though I have not acted since my schooldays, I threw myself into the part with zest. As the trial ended, and the murderer was set free by the jury of disreputable minor miners (average age 6 years), I walked back on to Main Street, now draped in velvety night. Looking down the street, fairly dimly lit even today, it is easy to picture the ghosts of horses, carts, and stagecoaches clattering about, and the rowdy, boisterous crowds that were the lifeblood of Deadwood. Rarely has a town been so inaccurately named!

Clockwise from top left: Buffalo Bill's room at the historic Franklin Hotel, Deadwood; John Wayne's room at the Franklin Hotel; the original "Herbie" permanently housed at the Celebrity Hotel, Deadwood; original historic photograph of the main street of Deadwood Gulch; grave of Calamity Jane; the infamous Dead Man's Hand, held by Wild Bill when he was assassinated; grave of Wild Bill Hickok at Mount Moriah Cemetery, Deadwood.

Clockwise from top: Enactment of trial of Wild Bill's murderer, Jack McCall; original Saloon No.10, site of the murder of Wild Bill Hickok; fateful Lodge Trail Ridge, over which the feckless Fetterman was decoyed by Crazy Horse, broods over the remains of Fort Phil Kearney; deeply ironic historic poster at Crook County Museum, Sundance; sculpture of the Sundance Kid in Crook County Jail.

DAY 24: 13 JUNE - ONE FOR THE UNDERDOG; ZERO FOR HUBRIS

It was the first long drive after a week of loafing around the Black Hills. I left sleeping Deadwood early. Its tourism slogan, "Deadwood Alive!" does not refer to mornings! In search of breakfast, I headed hopefully into the next town, Spearfish. And searched and searched and searched. This is probably how brunch got invented – you keep hunting for breakfast until near lunchtime. Though I left the beautiful Black Hills reluctantly, I looked forward to rendezvous with my wife at Cody, Wyoming in a few days. It had been a long, lonely month. Before then, my dashing, new-look beard simply has to go!

After all this time, the disembodied voice of the Garmin lady has become a dear, familiar friend, and I feel almost a physical reluctance to disobey her instructions, for fear of hurting her feelings. Only occasionally has she led me astray. This entire area was originally Dakota Territory, and only much later divided into North & South Dakota. It has been the land of the Dakotas for centuries, since they migrated west across the Missouri onto the high plains.

After brunch, I was back on my old friend I-90, passing the "Centre of the Nation", at Belle Fourche. To my continuing puzzlement, the geographic center of the USA is, supposedly, in South Dakota though I cannot figure out how. I stopped briefly at the Vore Buffalo Jump to have a look at the place the Lakota of old chased bison over a cliff, to kill them without expending arrows or bullets.

Drifting through little Sundance (not, as their literature points out, where the film festival is), I dropped by the Crook County courthouse, where the Sundance Kid went on trial and the jail from which he escaped 18 months later to join Butch Cassidy and the Hole in the Wall Gang, transforming Harry Longabaugh into that darling of Hollywood, The Sundance Kid. Together, they would go on the biggest and longest crime spree in the history of the West. It would emerge only much later that some crimes attributed to him were really committed by large ranchers out to annex nearby lands illegally. Tucked away in the little basement is a surprisingly rich haul of historic artifacts, at the Crook County Museum. I am told there are plans to shift it to a more appropriate location in the vaguely distant future. Outside is an evocative sculpture of the Kid, lounging nonchalantly in his jail cell. Notch up one more sighting of Frontier heritage.

As I head deeper into lovely Wyoming, full of hills and little lakes, snowy peaks appear on the horizon, a reminder that the approaching, beautiful Montana lives up to its name. Traffic is very light; the few vehicles I do pass are mostly RVs. One man I see has taken his entire house along! I give that Wide Load a wiiiide berth, remembering the incident with the car carrier near Bear Butte.

Meanwhile, I have added a few more, choice roadside signs to my collection. “Crazy Woman Creek” must have an interesting story. Then comes “Force Road” – persuasion did not work, huh? Most States post sharply reduced speed limits in road work areas, warning of doubled fines, but South Dakota tries gentle humor instead, requesting “Our workers...give ‘em a brake.” I happily do.

Two and a half hours out of Sundance, I ride into Fort Phil Kearny. This famous Fort, intrinsically linked to Red Cloud’s glory days as well as Crazy Horse’s early years, is a poignant sight. Once the US Army surrendered it to Red Cloud, after two years of failing to win

Red Cloud's War, it was burnt to the ground by his warriors along with the other abandoned Forts along the Bozeman Trail. This was the largest of the stockade forts on the Bozeman Trail, enclosing 17 acres of land with an eight-foot wall made of over 4000 logs. All that remains today is a wide field of lovely wildflowers in a valley surrounded by green pine ridges, marked by rusting signs bearing mute testimony to past lives and spilled blood.

The site was remarkably badly chosen for a fort, as the soldiers had no option but to travel miles over open ground to collect wood and water, exposing them to Red Cloud's warriors. At the Visitor Centre, the Ranger video, like the one at the Washita, does credit to the country with its complete balance and honesty, despite it being an embarrassing disaster for the Army. There is just one half-hearted attempt to explain away the Army's shattering defeat as being due to the soldiers using muzzle-loading guns, which fired just once in the time it took a warrior to shoot six arrows. However, it rightly claimed the Lakota had never carried out planned ambushes before.

As I drove the barely two miles up and over the fateful Lodge Trail Ridge, I could easily visualize the scene that unfolded here. The soldiers' horses charged up the green Ridge, snorting and panting, urged on with overconfident battle cries. The few Lakotas ahead were clearly fleeing in panic. It must have appeared too easy a kill to resist. Summitting, Captain William Fetterman barely paused to consider his Commander's specific orders, repeated not once but thrice, not to cross this very Ridge, well aware as he was of the danger of ambush beyond.

With the arrogance of inexperience, Fetterman contemptuously threw caution to the winds and dashed over. As he had bragged repeatedly, with just 80 troopers he could wipe out the entire Lakota Nation – and his squad numbered exactly 80. As they plunged headlong into the valley and up a little rise beyond, suddenly, seemingly rising out of the very earth, several hundred furious warriors sprang out of hiding – exactly as Colonel Carrington had forewarned the feckless Fetterman. In short order, they wiped out the entire troop, down to the last man. Known to the Lakota as the Battle of the Hundred in Hand, it was the Army's worst defeat till Custer outdid the ignominy several times over, exactly ten years later. Red Cloud led the Fetterman Fight. To head up the decoy party, which so convincingly lured the soldiers on, he appointed an upcoming young warrior of destiny, Crazy Horse. It was the beginning of a war career that remains unmatched in the annals of American history. Score one – a big one – for the underdog. Today, large cut-outs of Lakota warriors stand silently watchful on the crest of the Ridge and, from the Fort, it is not difficult to visualize Red Cloud's fighters there, looking down on the beleaguered garrison.

A little path led across the Ridge to the small crest where the fight took place. About to step down that path to visit the hillock, I noticed the familiar rattlesnake warning and, just like that, decided I did not *really* need to go there after all, since I could see it perfectly well from where I was! What led a trained officer to flagrantly disobey orders and end up with his entire command killed? It seems to have been the same factors that influenced Custer – overweening ego and unbridled ambition though, in Custer's case, he did not have the excuse of inexperience. Custer, too, had famously boasted he could "whip all the Indians on the Continent with the 7th Cavalry." He, too, would learn the error of his ways, though too late. The Lakota warriors skilfully forced Fetterman's troops to split into three fragments and mopped them up, like swatting flies. At the Little Bighorn, Custer would himself split his soldiers up into three prongs, resulting in his entire troop also being wiped out. The price of hubris is heavy indeed.

It would take the Army years to understand that the Natives fought as they hunted, relying on tactics rather than technology. However, once they learned guerrilla warfare from the Lakota, the tide would turn inexorably. For the Natives, living and fighting had always been both individual and personal. Their highest honor was to touch a live enemy, in a bold display of personal courage, rather than killing him. Hence, the understandable claim by the Army that the defeat was because the Lakota changed tactics unexpectedly. It had never known them to fight a planned, tactical battle. The Army still had not understood the Lakota warrior code, "Every day is a good day to die."

After pondering these thoughts for an hour, I headed the five winding miles, through lovely tree cover, following roads of loose gravel on which my car skated along erratically like a happy schoolgirl, to the site of the Wagon Box Fight, which took place the year following the Fetterman debacle. Strange, I thought, that the road to the Army's embarrassment is a smooth, paved, welcoming one, while the one to the Army's victory, sort of, is a rough and ready one. Somebody does not seem to care too much for the Army!

Here the tables turned, at least partially. The soldiers used the dismounted chassis boxes of their covered wagons to form a protective corral and, critically, unknown to the Lakota, used the Army's new, far-shooting, rapid-repeating rifles for the first time. This resulted in a standoff, and it eventually forced Red Cloud to pull back. In his last days, he would admit to losing half his warriors here. The carcass of one wagon box still lies in that grassy field, a mute marker of their defensive circle. Strangely, the Ranger video omits this Army semi-victory, while it covers the Fetterman defeat thoroughly.

Exhausted by a fascinating day, I finally arrived at the adorable little Story Pines Inn and relaxed on its front lawn, watching wild deer wander about the grassy verge. A fairy-tale wishing well among the flowers and the soothing sound of wind-chimes on the breeze lulled me – till a heavy pine-cone fell on my head! Now I have some appreciation for Newton. The environment was immensely soothing, the Inn small and homey, the service extraordinarily personalized and caring. Their booking confirmation had allocated me their "Welcome to Paradise Room 2." Inside, the furnishings were of natural, local pine. That evening I finally learned how to run a coin laundry, WITH detergent!

The next morning, I discovered that my hosts, Paula and Patrick Morgan had, with amazing thoughtfulness, cleaned the dirt and dew off my car's windshield for me. The little Rajasthani mirror-work pen I gave her, as a souvenir, seemed such an inadequate thank you. Despite having traveled extensively around the world for work and pleasure, I have never experienced such amazing hospitality and wished it was not such an out-of-the-way place and that I could be sure of returning someday. Sadly, I am unlikely to be back this way. Thank you for an unforgettable stay, little Story Pines Inn and the magnificent Morgans.

I asked Paula to recommend restaurants nearby, and she suggested two. A quick coin flip settled on the Wagon Box Restaurant, a half-mile down the road. It turned out to be in a beautiful stand of tall trees, with a bar and large outdoor dining patio. On such a lovely evening, it was almost full but, after checking with the barmaid, I snagged a table near the center of the patio. Then, after 24 magical days on the trail, when I least expected it, I realized racism is still alive and well in some dark little corners. For the next half an hour, the young server just did not notice me at all, perhaps because my skin blended into the brown, wooden furniture. Debating simply walking away, I decided to press the issue instead and returned to the barmaid to ask her, bluntly, if their waitress had a problem serving me. To her credit, her colleague's behavior embarrassed her, and she immediately sent the errant girl out to me. The owner, sitting with friends nearby, must have noticed, as she immediately came over to make up for her server's misbehavior, graciously serving me herself, which went a long way to mollify me. Fortunately, the food was outstanding and, despite this unpleasantness, I enjoyed my meal. When it came time to pay, the racist server tried to make nice, realizing it was tip time. It was too little, too late. She received exactly the tip she deserved. Beautiful Story, and the lovely Wagon Box Restaurant, really do not deserve this little drop of poison.

DAY 25: 14 JUNE - GLORY IN SUNSET

Battle waged furiously in the expansive valley of the Rosebud River, under the indifferent gaze of the Wolf Mountain. Vastly out-manned and considerably outgunned, Crazy Horse had ridden through the dark night with his small band of 700 hand-picked warriors and attacked General George Crook's army of 1300 at first light (the Montana State Parks brochure incorrectly claims they were of "about an equal number"). Among Crook's teamsters was the irrepressible Calamity Jane, disguised as a man. The warriors were fighting to defend their camp, over the watershed on the Little Bighorn River. At the peak of the battle, a Cheyenne Chief, Comes in Sight, had his horse shot from under him and it catapulted him to the ground. His sister, Buffalo Calf Road Woman, watching from a nearby ridge, immediately grabbed a horse and charged fearlessly to his rescue. Collecting him on the gallop, she rode back to their own lines, unscathed. Forever thereafter to the Natives, this battle on the Rosebud would be The Battle Where the Girl Saved Her Brother. It was a prime example of the fearless warrior spirit that infuses Native women, just as much as it does their men.

Largely with bows and arrows or old percussion relics and fur trade fusils, against the Army's massed modern, repeating weaponry, it should have been as futilely heroic as the Polish Army's horse cavalry charges against German tanks at the start of World War II. It was the world of values and spirituality versus the world of realpolitik. Amazingly, against all the odds, Crazy Horse defeated

General Crook, forcing him to retreat, eventually all the way back to Fort Robinson.

As a result, neither he nor General Terry would be on hand to support, or control, Custer a week later. Afterward, an estimate showed that this battle cost the US Government $1 million for each Native warrior killed. The overall cost of the entire Indian Wars would be an astronomical $150,000 per day. Buying peace, instead, would have been a bargain. It is ironic that this, his only ever defeat by Natives, was inflicted on General George Crook, a rare intellectual in the military who understood and empathized with the Natives. He probably never forgave Crazy Horse this defeat as, in the fateful days to come, he allegedly supported the military plot to imprison the peacefully surrendered Chief and exile him to a wretched Florida island, indirectly leading to his assassination.

Despite being such a landmark battle – and despite Montana charging visitors $6 (under an unmanned, honor system) for the pleasure of trying to figure its elements out for themselves – the Rosebud site is sadly neglected, with few visitors. To explore the battlefield fully, one really needs a 4x4 vehicle and sadly, my little Ford complained so vigorously that I had to desist after a couple of miles of barely visible, weed and prairie grass overgrown, track. There are few interpretive signs around, and the little narrative that there is made a very half-hearted attempt to claim the Army won this battle, while also, amusingly, making it abundantly clear that that is the Army's view and not that of the Parks Service! I wondered, if the Army really won, why did General Crook, with a far larger force and the overwhelming superiority of arms, withdraw completely from the area, ensuring he would not be on hand to reinforce Custer and act as the crucial element in Sheridan's pincer strategy. I located the exact spot where the girl saved her brother, visible through the improvised telescope of a piece of hard plastic tubing bored at eye-level into a wooden post, pointing to the place.

My faithful Garmin, too, seemed to have picked up the Montana attitude to Rosebud as it routed me, without my realizing it, via a strange road that ensured I missed seeing the Cheyenne

Museum at the St. Labre Indian School in Ashland, and also the historically significant town of Lame Deer. Then, it suddenly shut down altogether – though it did eventually return to life, equally mysteriously, and carried on as though nothing had happened. They say Orientals are inscrutable, but they are an open book compared to the strange workings of technology!

A week later the arrogant, overly ambitious Custer, blind to all realities except the fantasy of his own invincibility and glory, divided his utterly exhausted troops into three separate detachments. With his own 250 soldiers, he attacked a camp of 1500 skilled warriors under veteran war chiefs, forever immortalized as the Battle of the Little Bighorn or, to the Lakota, the Battle of the Greasy Grass. Custer, like Fetterman, blatantly ignored General Terry's repeated instructions of caution and explicit orders to coordinate with all the other units. That would have risked credit for his 'victory' being snatched by someone else. During a survey expedition, early in his career, in 1873, his commanding officer had noted witheringly, that Custer was "a cold-blooded, untruthful and unprincipled man... universally despised by all the officers of his regiment."

In a characteristic blunder, he had refused General Terry's offer of more troops. Had he not always claimed his 7th Cavalry alone was enough to destroy the entire Lakota Nation? He expected to repeat his Washita tactic, wanting, at any cost, his 'victory' to occur in time for him to make a bid for nothing short of the Presidency of the United States, at the upcoming Democratic National Convention. Strangely, he not only split his force, but he also forced his soldiers and horses, too exhausted to even stand, to immediately join battle. Even their enemies found their plight pitiful, as Sitting Bull confirmed later, "They were brave men, but they were just too tired." Custer was well known for his ridiculous exaggerations to the media, as confirmed by modern reviews by the US Army itself, and it is possible that, by this stage, he had convinced himself that those heroic, almost superhuman tales he spun of his imagined victories were true. His past 'fights' in the Indian Wars had been almost entirely with women, children and old men. However here, he faced not peaceful, defenseless old Black Kettle, but the genius of Crazy Horse, inspired by the vision of Sitting Bull.

Crazy Horse was the first on the battlefield to realize Custer's preferred strategy was to pursue defenseless non-combatants. Custer attacked knowing almost nothing of his enemy, the size of its force, its positions or intentions, while Crazy Horse refused to commit any of his forces till he knew exactly when, where and how Custer would attack. Early in his war career, Crazy Horse had understood that once Army units were isolated and their command structure broken, they were finished, unlike Native warriors who fought as individuals to the end. Hence, he always tried to eliminate enemy leadership. Nowhere would this tactic work more effectively than on the Little Bighorn.

As Chief Gall chased the retreating Custer up Last Stand Hill, Crazy Horse, anticipating his every move, completely out-generalled him and, despite only one in five of his warriors possessing guns, outflanked him and turned the retreat into a complete rout, systematically wiping both Custer and his entire command off the face of the earth. This would rank with the 1791 Battle of Wabash as the worst defeat of the US Army at the hands of the Native Nations.

The Achilles' Heel of any military, the unbounded hubris of an unsuitable commander, invariably costs the lives of hapless soldiers. One side led by a man who graduated dead last in his class at West Point, at the head of soldiers trained for a mode of warfare that was not relevant here, fighting for a salary and spoils; the other side, led by two of the greatest Native American war chiefs of all time, leading warriors trained almost from infancy to fight, and do so with reckless bravery and fearlessness, for honour and not any material goods. It was a textbook case of underestimating the enemy. In fairness, it was probably also the first time that any Native American war chief had been able, through the sheer force of his personality and reputation, to persuade his warriors to follow him away from the battle in front of them and around a hill to a critical, unseen opportunity. That was the decisive factor in the battle. As one of his surviving opponents would later agree, with his brain he positioned his warriors perfectly; with his courage, he won the battle. They say, for the Lakota, the fight at Last Stand Hill was similar to hunting buffalo.

Every time I think of these events, the Grand Entry at almost all pow-wows, where Veterans parade in with a US flag, seems so utterly incongruous and jarring. How the times have changed. Never before, or after, were the Lakota so united or so ably led. The quiet, modest, non-materialistic, personally unambitious Crazy Horse, the antithesis of Custer in every way, was the decisive factor in the battle, just as Sitting Bull's inspirational vision, coming out of his recent Sun Dance, was the decisive factor in uniting and motivating the Lakota and Cheyenne to their greatest victory ever. However, even in that moment of glory, the wise old chiefs knew it was their last hurrah. America would have to respond with massive force, and the Lakota were already in twilight. Doubtful of their ability to win militarily, the Army would use its might, instead, to drive the buffalo to near extinction, forcing the Natives to near starvation. Hunger finally won the West. These free spirits would be forced, by the untrammeled greed of invaders, onto small reservations. In the end, America eradicated 95% of the Native population (compared to 63% of European Jewry that Hitler did). Genocide is, regrettably, defined by victors, not realities.

Atop Last Stand Hill, I gaze out over the prairie grass and dandelions swaying gently in the breeze. This is where the angry warriors "swarmed around like a river swirling around a rock." Today, it is a scene of extraordinary tranquillity, full of wildflowers nodding in the wind. The lonely, mournful klaxon of a passing long-haul rig sounds a dirge. The earth gently shrouds all remains of the bloody conflict. Even today, visitors are strictly forbidden metal detectors at the site, to ensure the dead rest in peace.

The fighting continued well after Custer's fall, as the Lakota mopped up the remnants of the hapless 7th Cavalry, but eventually, they began to slowly disperse in every direction, primarily because there was not enough food and grazing to sustain such a huge camp for long. The lush hillside is obscenely pockmarked with stark, white headstones, marking the place each soldier fell (Custer's is, perhaps fittingly, a contrasting black), which the US Army put up in 1890. However, it would not be until 1999, more than a hundred years after the white headstones were erected, that the National Parks Service installed red granite markers at the spots Native warriors perished. The monument to the doubtfully glorious 7th Cavalry, the same unit responsible for the Washita and Wounded Knee massacres, stands in isolation on that forlorn summit. A monument to all the Native tribes involved was finally installed only in 2003.

Attitudes have persisted, at least in some measure, as revealed in a story I read in a Native American magazine, not long after my somber visit to the Little Bighorn. A Lakota who had joined the modern-day 7th Cavalry – why on earth he chose to join that particular unit baffles me – was asked by his white fellow soldiers who won the Battle of the Little Bighorn. When he replied, truthfully, that it was Crazy Horse, he was soundly thrashed by his comrades and punished by his sergeant. It appears the 7th Cavalry, at least, is still allergic to the truth.

The Ranger video and lecture, understandably, tread lightly on the Army's "golden soldier," ignoring his rather glaring shortcomings. Subtly promoting the Army's version, it does not explain why its favorite son managed to get himself wiped out. A throng of white Americans (where are you, brown people?) pay homage to Custer. I, the sole Injun yet again, pay homage to Crazy Horse, Sitting Bull, and their warriors. Fortunately, the Crows, traditional enemies of the Lakota and, therefore, supporters of Custer, now operate an excellent excursion – Apsalooka Tour – of the expansive battlefield, offering a well-balanced narrative without grinding ancient axes. While our driver and one guide were Crows, the main narrator, who was an excellent storyteller, is a Texan adopted by the Crow. He provided a clear, even-handed and well-informed account of the wide-ranging battle, over many square miles, ending in Custer's Last Stand.

However, Custer was not the only commander who disgraced himself that day. Major Reno, commanding one of the three prongs of Custer's force, panicked after half his command died within the first few minutes of the battle – something they were utterly conditioned to believe could never happen, especially at the hands of Native warriors. The third commander, Captain Benteen, arrived after the battle was over, with little to do except bury the dead. The Apsalooka Tour narrative does try, ever so subtly, to downplay Crazy Horse's pivotal role in the battle, probably because the Crow suffered so many successful war parties led by him. Even today, the Crow guide answered my question candidly, there is still residual antagonism between the two peoples, though it is much muted from yesteryears.

I notice that Apasalooka Tours, realizing just how well-received their service has been, has quietly doubled their ticket price to a relatively hefty, though still very well worthwhile, $20. They seem more commercially savvy than the Lakota. Consistently siding with the colonizers against the Natives worked out very well for them in the end, as it allowed them to remain on their own land and prosper, unlike other tribes.

The death of the media's chimerical darling, Custer, shocked America and, as the Chiefs knew it would, spurred Congress to pour a torrent of troops and arms into the fight to finish the warrior Nations of the Great Plains. It was the beginning of the end of their entire way of life. The fabled heritage of the Great Plains was being wiped clear off the pages of history, and the finis would be Wounded Knee. Never would it see such glory again.

I am left wondering at a capricious universe that turned the Native Nations' greatest hour of glory, the second-most written about battle after Gettysburg, into the blood-red swansong of their world.

In 1926, a poignant ceremony took place on this gory battlefield. A nephew of Sitting Bull, named White Bull, and General Godfrey, both survivors of that fateful battle, met here, shook hands in peace, and ceremonially buried a hatchet. The name of the place, too, changed from Custer Battlefield Park to the Little Bighorn Battlefield.

The gift shop at the Battlefield, though operated by the Crow, on Crow land, is chockfull of items clearly labeled, "non-authentic Native American item"! That did not prevent them from pricing ambitiously. At their little cafe, I did – finally! – get to taste my first item of Native cuisine, the ubiquitous fry bread. It was delicious and reminded me a bit of our Indian naan.

Driving reluctantly away from the beautiful, remarkable hospitality of the Story Pines Inn that morning, I had stopped at the nearest McDonald, at Sheridan, for breakfast. God bless McDonald! I realized only now that I did not see a single one in the Black Hills. The service was exceptional. However, I could barely remain patient long enough to finish eating, knowing I was headed to the two big landmark battlefields. The snow-capped ranges in the distance played host to the usual lack of traffic and, also as usual, the total lack of people! At one point, zooming along the I-90, lonesome as an old bull buffalo on a hillside, I rounded a blind corner at 70 mph, and suddenly, faced an equally lonesome, disgruntled-looking black cow, right in the middle of the road, staring balefully directly at me! Fortunately, there was enough road still available for me to narrowly avoid converting her to steak. And my driving style improved considerably, thereafter. Further along, I saw several deer grazing peacefully beside the road, one even crossing fairly close to my car. As in Kansas, the freeway was, again, punctuated more by road-kill than milestones.

As a glorious multi-hued sunset colored the sky, I drove into Billings, not quite sure if it is a large town or a small city. My hotel was named Vegas, apparently geographically challenged. At last, in Billings, I located a Walmart and bought a pair of nail scissors. At this point in my trip, my claws would have been the envy of any passing grizzly! My thick, white beard completed that look.

Clockwise from top: Rosebud Battlefield, where the sister saved her brother; red markers when Native warriors fell, Little Bighorn; Native Memorial, Little Bighorn; White markers where soldiers fell, Last Stand Hill, Little Bighorn (black marker, appropriately, for Custer); 7th Cavalry Horse Cemetery, Last Stand Hill, Little Bighorn.

Clockwise from top: The blood-soaked fields of the Little Bighorn bask peacefully in the sun today; Sitting Bull's bow & arrows, from his surrender at Fort Yates, North Dakota; sculpture of Pony Express rider, outside the Buffalo Bill Center, Cody; author with month-old beard, before being shorn prior to wife's arrival at Cody; Schreyvogel's heart-wrenching "The Last Drop", the quiet dignity of true heroism.

DAY 26: 15 JUNE - HIPPIES & HELL'S ANGELS

A menacing biker gang followed me into my Cody motel. I eyed them apprehensively. They all had the regulation look – dauntingly decorated headgear and shades; black leather jackets; substantial physiques; the swagger. On closer inspection, there was the usual image confusion between hippie and Hell's Angel, with a dash of Easy Rider. I quickly escaped to my room, with relief, urban legends playing on my mind yet again.

Later in the evening, when they emerged from their rooms, the transformation was hilarious. The toughies had turned into paunchy old accountants, bandana free, grey hair neatly combed, fantasies done. Nightfall and a large U-Haul truck eased into the parking slot next to my car. By breakfast, it had vanished with the dew, and all the awesome Harleys transformed, like Cinderella's pumpkin coach, into mundane Toyotas and Fords. Yesterday's Hell's Angels had become today's aging retirees with wives - back to reality. Sigh!

The Bear Tooth Inn is, literally, at the edge of the runway of Cody's Lilliputian Yellowstone Regional Airport. It was a typical motel, offering a spacious room and beds and, thankfully, a good coffee maker and TV. It was also typical in its old, threadbare carpeting, undoubtedly harboring armies of unknown parasites, and a particleboard door that surely the termites would complete demolishing that very night. What was less typical was that it sandwiched the rooms between the car park and an internal corridor, with doors opening out to both. Also, unusual these days, it is American owned. It's okay - a brown alien is allowed to be a bit politically incorrect, now and then!

Moving north, I had passed many fish hatcheries, including a 'historic' one. What on earth could be historic about a fish hatchery? Interesting road signs gradually vanished – perhaps matching people's sense of humor? The passing scenery is reminiscent of the Scottish Highlands. The heavy overcast that had followed me from Billings, as I crossed from Montana back into Wyoming for the third time, finally delivered the long-promised Car Wash by Nature, cleansing miles of dust and insect splatter, just in time to welcome my wife, flying into Cody tomorrow. The town is tiny but has one priceless jewel that outshines all, the Buffalo Bill Centre of the West. Because of this, and its proximity to the Yellowstone National Park, even mediocre motels in Cody are substantially overpriced. And, for this, I would happily pay up again!

Even if it was not the eastern gateway to Yellowstone, this town would be worth visiting just for the fabulous, sprawling, five museum complex that is the Buffalo Bill Center of the West, set within a clutch of pretty gardens. At the ticket counter, I requested a regular ticket since, as I explained, I fell short of their Seniors qualifying age by a year.

He beamed and boomed, "Aw, never mind. I'll give it to you, anyway!"

That welcome, to me, is the difference in attitude between such institutions in America and almost anywhere else. As the saving was not insignificant, such attitudes make a Senior life much pleasanter!

Beautifully presented, bursting with fascinating collections, it is little wonder their somewhat pricey admission is valid for two days, not the usual one. I just wished I had two days in hand. Besides static exhibits, it has many experiential areas that magnetically draw in even non-museum enthusiasts. The Centre has also started a raptor rescue, taking in and caring for permanently injured large raptors. As I looked at her in awe, the beady-eyed Annie, their huge bald eagle, coolly assessed me for lunch.

The large Buffalo Bill Museum is, as expected, full of intriguing memorabilia of William 'Buffalo Bill' Cody and his world, such as an original Deadwood-Cheyenne Stagecoach (which Apaches had really attacked, an incident that he later staged in his shows), and documentary footage of his Buffalo Bill's Wild West Shows, which became such a craze across America and Europe in the early 1900s that even the redoubtable Queen Victoria could not resist demanding a command performance. Growing up in the West, Bill had played with Native children; as a Scout for the Cavalry, he had feared them, shockingly even scalping one; but later, as a showman, he came to know, understand and love them, kindling his unlikely friendship with the legendary Sitting Bull. This stressful split personality, between the Showman and the Frontiersman, eventually wearied him into retiring to a Ranch in the open countryside of the West that he loved so dearly.

Even more captivating is their Museum of the Plains Indians which, reflecting Buffalo Bill's later attitude to them, presents the story of the Plains Nations with unusual candor and honesty. The montages encourage you to step in, touch, experience. What must have appeared barbaric and savage to the simple-minded, Bible-thumping European migrants is compellingly explained in all its mystery and majesty.

It all reflects the Cody who said, "The Indians have been badly used. They have their side of the story. For honesty and virtue, I think the Indians are far ahead of the whites....They were here first, and have a better right to be here than we have."

Concurrently, it pays tribute to the sheer undaunted courage, hardiness, enterprise and tenacity of the pioneers - the extraordinary 'mountain men' fur trappers, who frequently assimilated into local tribes; the gold miners, greedy, unwitting saviours of the national treasury; the Chinese railroad men, unsung heroes belting together an entire Continent with iron track; the homesteading families, defying all the odds to turn millions of State-stolen acres agriculturally productive. With the inevitability of grinding tectonic plates, two vastly different civilizations mashed together here, ignited, and threw up the great and the ugly, and, ultimately, forged the greatest Nation the world has ever seen, the United States we know today. After the passage of centuries of pyrotechnics, hatred, and bigotry, the question remains whether it can become a kinder, gentler, more embracing, humane home for its indigenes. My heart beats an affirmation.

The Museum would not reflect America if it did not, as everywhere, have a huge gallery that is a temple to guns, fascinating women, it seems, as much as men. No others in the world have invented a greater variety of ingenious instruments for killing their fellow men. Even the sign, at the entrance to the Center, mildly advises checking that weapons carried in have their safeties on! Oh, America! Do you really expect to have to defend yourselves inside a museum, in remote, little Cody? I eye my fellow visitors with some concern.

A gallery I had especially wanted to visit contains their exceptional collection of the works of Frederic Remington, quintessential artist of the Old West. Many of his famous sculptures live on in glory here, as well as a mock-up of his Studio, a bizarre Wild West bubble in the heart of New York; bizarre even for a city where almost nothing is considered bizarre. His signature, washed-out pastel landscapes are displayed in all their splendor. The hours flew by, unnoticed, till an ominous rumble from my stomach reminded me that lunch was considerably overdue. The sun-kissed dining facility, sadly, had run out of the Elk Brat that I had wanted to try. I settled for more mundane fare.

I considered riding Cody's Trolley Tour but its exorbitant price shocked me. Moreover, I could not imagine there really being all that much to see in tiny Cody, anyway. And as for shoot-outs on the street, I had had my fill of them in Dodge City and Deadwood. There were inviting restaurants all along Sheridan Avenue which I could consider for dinner, but I think the month-long odyssey was finally beginning to take its toll on me or, perhaps, I was just feeling my age today. So, I just headed to my Motel.

Later that evening, resting in my room, I ordered a pizza from Dominos. It arrived, piping hot, in less than the promised half-hour and I got chatting with the delivery boy. With absolute certainty, he convinced me that, geographically, India is much larger than the United States!

DAY 27: 16 JUNE - TRAIL'S END

It rained again last night, scrubbing my car even cleaner, as I had hoped it would. But I pray the weather clears before my wife, Keya, arrives and we head up into the mountains, to Yellowstone. The morning had dawned the usual crisp 9 Celsius and I headed to breakfast. As I waited politely to enter the breakfast room, an English guest noticed me, this Colonial Massa deciding that I could only be a Motel Patel, haughtily informed me that his visiting daughter would also have breakfast.

Spitefully, just to pay him back for the presumption, I responded with a straight face, "No, I am afraid it is against State law."

Yes, terribly petty, but disgustingly satisfying! I am happily ashamed of myself.

Today, the Plains Indian Museum has a small pow-wow, at their Robbie Pow-wow Garden, and I am keen to drop in with my wife, neither of us ever having experienced one before. I notice that the Grand Entry is scheduled for noon and, checking on my wife's incoming flight, I find we will have just enough time to get there from the Airport. Perhaps we could have lunch there, eating genuine Native American delicacies and, I know, my wife would have an economic contribution to make to the many Native handicraft shops there.

At the Airport, I dropped a dollar into the honor jar and picked up my coffee, before sitting back to admire one of the tiniest airport terminals I have ever seen. At one point, just one person manned the Delta Airlines counter, scooting between Departures and Arrivals. Yes, it is that tiny!

Unlike the imperial hubris of Fraser's "End of the Trail" sculpture, I ride to my trail's end energetic and eager to experience the magic of Yellowstone – filled with a childhood diet of Yogi Bear and Booboo Bear of Jellystone. After a long, lone month, my wife now rides shotgun in my fossil-fuelled stagecoach, drawn by mechanical horses. The nearly three-hour drive to the center of Yellowstone is, to put it mildly, spectacular. Cody is passed in the blink of an unregretful eye, and right up to the gate of the National Park, it is about average on the wonder scale. Thereafter, suddenly, the road climbs into really breathtaking country, with a racing mountain river keeping us company along one side. Eventually, dramatic snowy peaks emerge on the skyline and, before you realize it, you are actually at the snowline. There is ice right beside the road – in summer! Traffic, unsurprisingly, is heavy but moves smoothly. Thoughtfully arranged pull-off areas at every scenic outlook enable you to stop and gawk, in awestruck wonder. I think of them as Gawk Gaps.

A very enjoyable two-and-a-half hours out of Cody, after innumerable oohs and aahs, we eventually make it to Grant Village on Yellowstone Lake, in the heart of the 9000 sq. km. protected wilderness and wildlife habitat that is the jaw-dropping Yellowstone National Park. I knew there were several Park tours available, but my wife and I agreed it would be much more fun to explore in our little car, spending a leisurely day in each area of the Park. That turned out to be a sage decision.

A pleasant and helpful Receptionist informed us that our room would be ready only at 4 pm and suggested various things we could do or see in the intervening three hours. We relaxed over a late lunch and then browsed the shops in the Village.

When we returned at 4 pm, we were in for a shock. A different Receptionist at the desk curtly barked that our room was not ready and didn't we know check-in was only at 4.30 pm. When I diffidently mentioned the other lady had given us the 4 pm time, she almost screamed, "Then she informed you incorrectly."

By then, it was already 4.26 pm, but she responded curtly, "But it's not 4.30, is it?"

So, we waited. She stared stonily at me till the four minutes ticked away and then slapped the room key onto the counter. On enquiring about a wi-if password she spat, "You have to pay for it." This is one of the very few places in the USA where you do.

What a welcome to the excitedly anticipated Yellowstone National Park.

DAY 28: 17 JUNE - THE STEAMING EARTH

Exhaustingly magnificent is probably the best way to describe the massive sprawl of the Yellowstone National Park. Scattered amid the expansive acres are several little villages of park lodges with cookie-cutter restaurants and shops. Some restaurants and dining rooms have stunning views. All the shops carry exactly the same, grossly sticker-shocking, uninspiring kitsch, while the menus at the dining rooms are as exorbitantly priced as I had expected, considering we were, literally, captive customers with nowhere else to go and no competition at all permitted within the Park. Just one entity operates everything, the peculiarly customer-unfriendly and aloof Xanterra Parks & Resorts. Service is slip-shod as the outlets are under-manned and overwhelmed.

I tried, at several locations, to file a formal complaint about the very rude Receptionist at Grant Village who handed us our key yesterday, but could not find a single means of doing this, other than an open, nondescript postcard addressed vaguely to Xanterra. While I mailed that in, I know it went directly towards filling an already overflowing garbage bin there.

The lodges at Grant Village are pretty, nestled amidst lush stands of pine, overlooking the lake. Their furnishings are adequate, but they have provided nothing beyond the absolute bare minimum. This seems to take "bear necessities" rather too literally!

The behavior of the Receptionist yesterday really dampened our spirits, but it only lasted the night. Though it dawned overcast and drizzly, we did not let that affect our enthusiasm for the grizzly and headed out early, to beat the crowds. And it rewarded us. Arriving at the Old Faithful Geyser, the amazing, huge, unbelievably punctual steam jet, the sporadic rain stopped, and we were in time to grab the best ringside seats for its next performance.

As we all waited, a condescending British tourist sitting beside us suddenly enquired whether we spoke Mandarin or Cantonese, trying to show off his knowledge that there are more languages in China than 'Chinese'. Discovering his "Chinese expertise" had let him down, and that we were, in fact, Indians, he was abashed for just a beat. Then, unfazed, he continued lecturing us, asking if we knew we were sitting on the world's biggest volcano which could erupt at any time. To his obvious chagrin, I confirmed we did and added that it would save us all cremation expenses, wouldn't it? He was not amused! In the course of further conversation, he discovered that my wife had studied in London and exclaimed, "That must have been an amazing experience for you."

I was so proud of her exquisitely cool put-down, "Well, after living for years in Switzerland, London was, I guess, interesting."

Exactly at 10.39 am, 90 minutes after its last eruption, Old Faithful began to build up a head of steam, and let loose with an utterly jaw-dropping display. In size, height and intensity it is everything it had been cracked up to be. What surprised us, though, was how quiet the eruptions are. Almost like a ballet, an entire troupe of subsidiary geysers accompanied this prima donna, letting off steam all around us. At the end of the performance, we wholeheartedly joined the audience in giving Old Faithful a rousing hand of applause!

Heading to Mammoth Hot Springs, near the northern entrance to the Park, we realized the entire area is a giant thermal basin, filled with innumerable steaming lakes, hot springs, and myriad geysers. Nearing Mammoth, the rain resumed, accompanied by a swirling mist, but nothing could dampen our excitement at the wild and wonderful spectacle. Because of the widespread, unusual thermal activity, there are strange rock formations all around among the ash that covers many of them like sand on a beach. The smell of sulfur in the air is strong, and I wondered if that had convinced the devoutly Christian early explorers that this is Hell.

Sections of the road were under repair, awash in mud which, once again, quickly camouflaged our car. On the way back, we tried the alternate route, via Canyon and Lake. This turned out to be a mistake as it was just boringly lovely, compared to the stunningly lovely route via Norris and Old Faithful.

However, we finally did get to say hello (from my wife, literally so!) to some wildlife. Massive buffalo (bison) grazed all around, completely ignoring the admiring hordes of tourists. Further down the road, we met a couple of elks, nonchalantly hanging out right next to the road. One carefully posed its behind for my wife's camera. I must confess I avoided eye contact with them, having just enjoyed elk sliders for lunch. Disappointingly, they had been mushy soft and generally only about okay. Nowhere near as tasty as buffalo, or beef; just okay.

And then, a grizzly attacked us! Just kidding – making sure you are still awake, reading this. Earlier, when we stopped at a pull-off near another motorist, he told us excitedly we had just missed seeing a grizzly. We all hung around for a while hoping it would return, but it was not to be. Perhaps tomorrow, we consoled ourselves, as we drove away. As if in sympathy, at that point, the heavens opened up again and a heavy thundershower ensued. Our little car, which had all but disappeared under its mud coating on the way up to Mammoth, now emerged again, washed sparkling clean. Even its radiator grille seemed to be smiling! We had thundershowers, on and off, most of the day, but did not let it rain on our parade. Yes, my Sons, too, groan at those Dad jokes.

Back at Deer Lodge, we decided to drown our sorrows at missing the grizzly, in a bottle of wine, completely forgetting we had picked up a corked bottle and, with unfathomable logic, there is no corkscrew at the Lodge. What ensued was a titanic struggle. But nothing gets between our wine and us! Pressed into service were car keys, scissors, coffee stirrers, patience, considerable perseverance, and ingenuity. The wine was drunk!

Clockwise from top left: East Gate of the Yellowstone National Park; a rushing river in Yellowstone; the Buffalo are finally returning to Yellowstone; the famous Yellow Bus of Yellowstone National Park; the Grand Canyon of the Yellowstone; Old Faithful in full cry, at Yellowstone National Park.

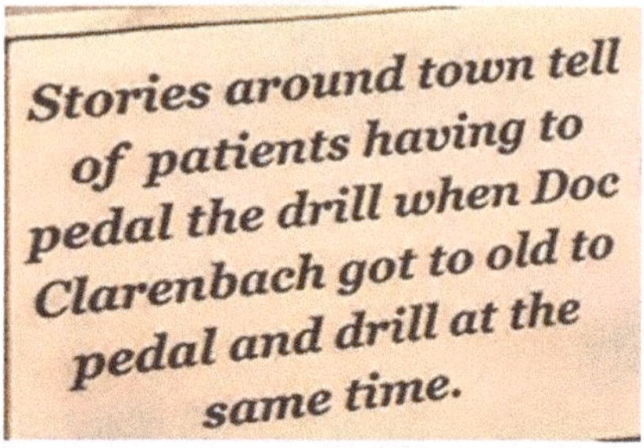

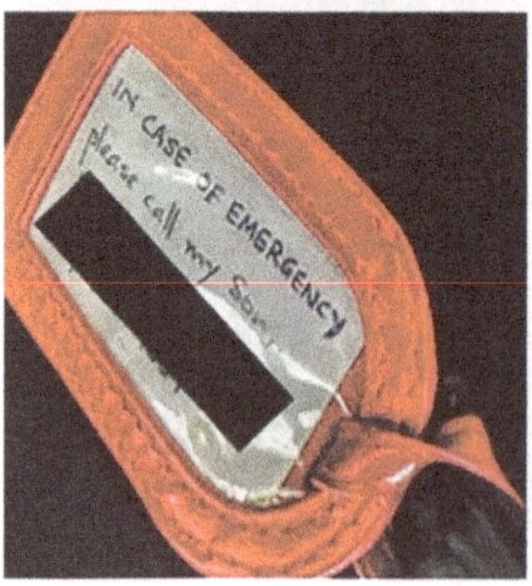

Clockwise from top left: Buffalo Bill's hunting lodge; summer in Yellowstone National Park!; dentistry in Cody, in them days; wild mustangs still roam the Rosebud Valley; Cherokee Stand Wattie was the last Confederate General to surrender; ready for any emergency; let's just take the entire house along!; Cody Airport tribute to the intrepid Mountain Men.

DAY 29: 18 JUNE - BEAR ENCOUNTER

It was another cold, rainy morning with the weather persisting, on and off, throughout the day. At 3 pm near Mount Washburn, the temperature in the car read 4 Celsius. So much for summer! Nothing daunted, we explored the route towards Roosevelt, up near the much-acclaimed North East Entrance to Yellowstone which is supposedly the scenic granddaddy of them all. As usual, our car soon vanished under its cloak of mud again. I hoped a good thunderstorm would come in overnight so I did not have to return a filthy car to Avis, at Cody airport, tomorrow.

The route from Canyon to Roosevelt fully lived up to its billing. It is, easily, the most beautiful and interesting road anywhere in the Park. As you drive up the mountain, the road becomes narrower and steeper, with hairpin bends bereft of any safety barriers. You cross the snowline and there is white all around – in summer! It looks like Switzerland. There is plenty of mist, clouds and steam vapor all over the place, creating an absolutely magical prospect.

Today turned out to be a lucky day for seeing wildlife, and we were fortunate enough to see a pair of black bear cubs gamboling on a hillside, playing hide-and-seek in the tall grass and climbing tree stumps. Their parents were somewhere close by, though camouflaged, and the ever-vigilant Rangers ensured no one got too adventurous in approaching them. Stoutly resisting the urge to take these bundles of cuteness home, since the Rangers might be unhappy, we moved on. Elk, bison, and moose were 'boringly' plentiful along the road, as we traveled north. Approaching the Upper Falls, we saw a line of stopped vehicles on the shoulder of the road, the certain sign that, we now knew, meant "Animal sighting!" Like any good rubbernecker, we squeezed our car in somewhere, somehow, defying the laws of physics, and ran to see what they were seeing. In the distance, we were rewarded with the sight of a pair of grizzly bears feeding leisurely, ignoring their human fan base on the hillside. Further on, we would pass another group of huge, black grizzlies fairly close to the road, but there was no place to stop there, even for the laws-of-physics-defying sorts. And there were several Rangers around to ensure no one even considered trying!

The Grand Canyon of the Yellowstone and the Upper Falls are incredibly awe-inspiring. The gorge is huge and wide, with a dizzying drop to the distant valley floor as the turbulent Yellowstone River cuts its millennia-old route through the mountains. There are several terrifying rapids and falls, including Tower Falls, a frighteningly powerful flood of water dropping a long, long way.

This sight considerably enhanced my respect for the old Mountain Men who navigated this river in their fragile little canoes, bringing beaver fur back for the demanding consumers on the East Coast. There was no way those men could have chosen this career just for the money – there were easier ways to make a living, even then. It was undoubtedly primarily for adventure and the primal machismo of man versus life-threatening Nature.

For lunch, at Roosevelt Lodge, I finally sank my fangs into a juicy, zesty bison steak, while my wife, despite my best efforts to persuade her, stuck with a less adventurous rack of ribs. For us both, however, this enormous meal resulted in our deciding, come evening, to make a dinner of just wine and a few crackers! While we rested from our culinary labors on the wooden porch of the Roosevelt Lodge, in a happy meat stupor, a rare fox trotted gracefully by. It was here, at Roosevelt, that my wife finally had her long-cherished wish granted – she finally saw some Rangers wearing the dimpled hats made famous by our childhood Yogi Bear comics!

The change in the weather seemed to have cheered the animals too. We passed several huge grizzly bears moving leisurely about. It was not a place we could stop safely so, really thrilled to have glimpsed them, even in passing, we moved on. A little further, Rangers had stopped traffic to allow part of a herd of bison to cross the road, as they had decided the grass on the other side was greener. Finally, a Ranger shooed a small baby bison, scampering on unsteady legs, back to its mother.

Near Fishing Bluff, in the middle of a field, another fox stood stock still, peering fearlessly at the passing cars.

DAY 30: 19 JUNE - TOKSHA AKHAY

This will be the last entry in my diary for this epic, personal pilgrimage. I know I will never again have such an extraordinary adventure in this lifetime. My amazing odyssey is finally over. I stored a lifetime of wonder in my mind, for "reflection in tranquillity."

Yellowstone was the perfect capstone. It is one of the most strange and beautiful places on earth. On our penultimate day, we delighted in discovering the Canyon to Roosevelt road, easily the most exciting and diverse part of this giant wilderness. We passed huge Yellowstone Lake, with a strange, narrow island hosting a stand of mature trees, right out on the water. The next act was Mud Volcano, an entire area of heaving thermal activity, with clouds of steam constantly billowing out of the boiling mud everywhere, and an overpowering sulphuric smell in the air. It was Dante's inferno! The snowline, at just over 8000 feet, transmuted it into the Swiss Alps. The most dramatic, however, had been the Grand Canyon of the Yellowstone, through the Absaroka Range.

On our final morning, we again headed out early, for Cody Airport, hoping to see more wildlife. As they materialized out of the mists, like disembodied ghosts, we virtually ignored the passing elk and bison, having become a bit blasé by then. A lone deer made a cameo appearance before bouncing away. My wife drove for a while, but then I took over the wheel again as she was a far better wildlife spotter than I. Then, we were truly blessed. Just ahead, loping slowly along beside the road, was a huge, adult black bear.

Glancing warily back at us every so often, it continued along, right beside us, for quite a while, before ambling into the trees.

Breakfast was at Buffalo Bill's original wooden hunting lodge, Pahaska Tepee, just outside the park gates. A beautiful place, with good food, and service with a smile, it even had a genuinely good gift shop, reasonably priced. There are wooden cabins here for overnight guests and, I realized, it would have been a far better alternative to spending the night in Cody.

All too soon, the mountains dumped us onto the plains at their feet. Our magical interlude was over.

The cheerful Avis girl at Cody Airport happily accepted our keys, without even glancing at the car, its mileage, fuel level or anything at all. She just accepted the keys on trust, an act that impressed us, and converted us to long-term Avis fans. Here is one car rental agency, or perhaps just the one location, where you are a guest, rather than a suspicious scamster trying to rip the agency off somehow. Bravo, Avis Cody Airport!

Our tiny feeder aircraft from Cody landed in Salt Lake City for the transfer to its big mama counterpart. As we deplaned, I noticed the jetway to the gates was unusually low to the ground, very different from anything I have seen anywhere. We boarded the larger Boeing and settled in, happy to have more legroom than the previous flight, but after half an hour of meditating peacefully in our seats, the pilot cheerfully informed us that there was a problem with the aircraft and we would have to transfer to another. Eventually, this was done fairly efficiently by Delta and we departed Salt Lake City, the headquarters of the Mormons, just an hour behind schedule. We accepted the delay philosophically, well-conditioned by the fact that, on arrival in San Francisco, the inevitable scrum over the Bay Bridge to the East Bay would take us almost twice as long.

As the flight banked over the serene glory of the Bay Area, making its final approach to San Francisco International, I reflected on the entire experience. Overcoming the horrors of the past, there is definitely a slowly dawning revival among the Native Americans of the Great Plains. I am confident Wakan Tanka will inspire this great, awe-inspiring country, of such heroic achievements and dynamism, to finally embrace them, and the great American Dream will become an inclusive reality. An old Lakota saying cautions, “We will be known forever by the tracks we leave behind” – mainstream America needs to decide whether its tracks will reflect a truly great civilization or one that is shackled in genocide. “We, the People” must include ***all*** the people.

Toksha Akhay, till we meet again - in this life or the next.

AFTERWORD

A major English newspaper in the Sultanate of Oman had accepted my proposal for a daily column "from the road," as I drove my unusual quest, and offered me generous space on its pages. I was pleased to have this opportunity to share my experiences with others and did not bother to enquire about remuneration, knowing all publications have fixed rates for contributions.

The 22 long despatches duly appeared, faithfully reproduced over many column inches each day from my wired articles, and hopefully, some folk even read them. On my return to Oman, when I routinely requested the payment due for them, they told me they do not pay for guest columns, instead offering me "exposure"! This was the first such experience in all my years of freelancing, and it left me to wonder at what possible exposure I could benefit from, at this stage in my life and career. Unfortunately, I had only myself to blame as I had not thought it necessary to check on this aspect of things before setting out on my adventure. Ruefully, I acknowledged a lesson in the vagaries of the newspaper world in our Region.

As I sit contemplatively in the peaceful twilight of my study in Muscat, I visualize a drone's eye view of the story of the Great Plains. In the end, the honors – an obscene context for the word – of the Native American Wars came down about even, with approximately 20,000 dead on either side, the Native cemeteries filled with large numbers of women, children and the elderly; the Army cemeteries almost exclusively with the remains of once heavily armed soldiers.

The US Army, it seems, perhaps more than any other fighting force in history, has always been profligate with the lives of its rank and file – a trend visible even in its never-ending conflicts of the 21st Century – a damning waste of youth, potential, and hope in a nation that could use them to lead the world. On the one side were warriors trained for battle almost from infancy, steeped in the traditions of personal bravery and honor above all else, fighting guerrilla wars in infinitely familiar terrains, powerfully driven to save their homes, people and way of life. On the other side were mercenary fighters, frequently compelled by unfortunate personal histories, driven over the water from Europe by starvation and desperation, riding terrain-unfit mounts, trying to fight classic European set-piece battles in utterly unfamiliar and hostile geographies, often under leaders motivated more by personal ambition and vainglory than national interest, driven by gold, coveting the lands of strangers who had shown them hospitality and welcome on their arrival in a strange land.

In the broad sweep of human history, it has to be one of the most one-sided clashes of civilizations ever, on many levels. Great as the tragedy of the past is, even more appalling is that it compels the Native Nations to suffer the aftershocks to this very day.

It is best expressed by Peter Matthiessen, "In the Spirit of Crazy Horse," when he states, "Our nostalgia comes easily, since these stirring people are safely in the past, and the abuse of their proud character, generosity and fierce honesty – remarked upon by almost all the first Europeans to observe them – can be blamed upon our roughshod frontier forebears."

Eventually, it was not the endless torrent of men and materiel of the US Army that defeated the Native Nations, but the ruthless scorched earth policy that wiped the buffalo almost completely off the face of the Great Plains, confronting the indigene with the stark choice of watching his family starve to death, or accepting reluctant sustenance from the uncertain and untrustworthy hand of the invader, a dependence that, like a thorn deeply embedded in the flesh, cannot be excised but with considerable pain and blood.

Eventually, the story of the Great Plains will not be written in death and defeat. The most glorious chapter of all, the revival of the Buffalo Nations, like the revival of the buffalo itself from the very edge of extinction, is yet to be written. It is the time of the seventh generation.

LAKOTA WORDS USED IN THIS BOOK

Akicita : traditional Lakota tribal police
Canku Luta : Red Road
Cante wasta upo : welcome with an open heart
Hanble-ceya : crying for a vision
Heyoka : holy clowns, inspired by the thunder beings
Kola : brother
Mahapiya Luta : Red Cloud
Maka unchi : grandmother Earth
Mato Paha : Bear Butte
Mitakuye oyasin : we are all one
Paha Sapa : Black Hills
Pila maya : thank you
Skan : choice
Tasunko Witko : Crazy Horse
Tatanka Yotake : Sitting Bull
Thievo : white man (in Comanche)
Toksha akhay : farewell till we meet again
Wakan Tanka : Great Spirit / Great Mystery / Unknowable Great
Wakinyan : thunder beings
Wanbli Tokahe : Leading Eagle
Wasicu : white man (literally, the greedy one)
Wasicu Wakan : holy white man
Wicasa Wakan : holy man / medicine man
Wicasa Itancan : Chief

A FEW LITTLE KNOWN FACTS

- The largest concentration of pyramids in the world is not in Egypt, but near St. Louis. The largest of these, at Cahokia, is considerably larger than the Pyramid of Khufu in Egypt, and the city was larger than London in 1250 AD. Their large cities show they were not just nomadic hunter-gatherers but had a very advanced, ancient civilization. It is a glaring reflection on commentators like de Tocqueville who claimed, "They were prevented from developing a civilization by their implacable prejudices, their uncontrolled passions, their vices..."

- The Lakota language does not have any curse words, nor any words for "owning the land."

- All the geographic places, landmarks and features in America so dramatically "discovered" by white explorers over the years, were all shown to them by local Native guides, who had 'discovered' them millennia earlier. Even Cortez may never have 'discovered' the Aztecs but for a traitorous Native woman with a grudge against her people.

- The Pilgrims from the Mayflower survived only with the help of the Wampanoag tribe, who gave them food and taught them about the local flora. In return, the settlers killed their

Chief, Metacon, and sold his wife and son as slaves, for 30 pieces of silver.

- Native Nations traded and traveled freely and frequently, from Canada to South America, in an ancient NAFTA, from the hunter-gatherers of the North (Aleuts, Innuits) to the huge urban centers of the South (Maya, Inca, Aztec). Then, the great Native cities suddenly and inexplicably vanished and people moved to small villages.

- The 14th Amendment of the US Constitution abolished slavery for African-Americans, but not for Native Americans. That happened only as late as 1924.

- Christopher Columbus and his son were both slavers, who actively captured, enslaved, and traded Natives. They never set foot on the American mainland.

- Contrary to Hollywood myths, in over 4000 films, scalping was unknown to the Natives till the Spanish, and other white settlers began this practice for tallying bounties for Natives killed.

- Misunderstanding of Native words sometimes led to amusing names, e.g. the Algonquin "Chicago" means "place of smelly weeds"; the Muskogean "Tallahassee" means "abandoned town"; the Cree "Winnipeg" means "dirty water". The Spanish called the entire Continent "Florida".

- The legendary hero Kit Carson was, in reality, a turncoat. For many years he lived with the Arapaho and Cheyenne, adopted their ways, and even had a child by one of their women. Then, to curry favor with the Army, he betrayed them without hesitation, executing the Army's scorched earth policy with ruthlessness, killing thousands of non-combatants.

- Blatant disregard for international law and jurisdiction was a sad hallmark of US policy even then. Two major Santee War Chiefs were kidnapped from well inside Canada and executed after a dummy trial. Even a partisan, white newspaper, the St. Paul "Pioneer," observed, "We do not believe serious injustice will be done by this execution, but it would have been more credible if some tangible evidence of their guilt had been obtained."

- Denver is one of the many modern cities built on land stolen from the Natives, guaranteed to them by legally valid Treaties in force even today.

- Ely Parker, a Seneca Native, wrote the terms of the Confederate surrender, for Ulysses Grant, at Appomattox, as he had the best English handwriting of anyone assembled there.

- Native Americans did not receive the rights of citizenship, in their own land, until 1924.

- "Termination" of Native lands, under "eminent domain" continued right up to the term of President Eisenhower. President Kennedy was the first leader to heed their issues; President Obama the first, and only one, to apologize to them.

- The original Native population is estimated to have been around 18 million. By 1900, it had been reduced to 0.25 million, i.e. 98% exterminated, through an explicit State policy of genocide. For example, General Patrick Conner is on record as having ordered, "You will not receive overtures of peace or submission from Indians, but will attack and kill every male Indian over twelve years of age." In comparison, Hitler killed 63% of European Jewry. Today, the Native population has recovered to around 5 million. However, large numbers of them are still disenfranchised because of political gerrymandering.

- Even today, the 60 year Indian War is the longest war fought by the US in its history. Despite the Army's vast superiority of arms and numbers, a shockingly similar 20,000 died on either side and cost the US well over $150,000 per day, an eloquent tribute to the Natives' fighting skills and tenacity.

- The concept of an elected "Chief," as we know it, is a Western invention. Native warriors fought for individual honor. They selected leaders on merit only – bravery, excellence in battle, vision, care for their people. Warriors followed someone by choice, not a mandate. 'Skan', choice, is something every human has and no Native would ever deny it or try to force it on anyone else. The truest democracy/meritocracy.

- The Iroquois Confederacy was a democracy when Europe was ruled by hereditary kings and despots. The visiting Benjamin Franklin was so impressed by their system that he incorporated some elements into the new US Constitution.

- When Europe was starving, Columbus brought back corn, potatoes, and beans from the Native Americans. The cultivation of these three crops, arguably, saved swathes of Europe.

- Over 150 years ago, Black Elk's vision recorded the coming dangers of climate change and environmental pollution, which is evident today.

- The tepee always belonged to the woman, and to divorce a husband, all she had to do was to put his moccasins outside the tepee.

- The Wampanoag had an annual Thanksgiving for centuries. The Pilgrims borrowed the idea, after enslaving and slaughtering these benefactors.

- The Vatican's iniquitous "Doctrine of Discovery" justified European Christians' theft of indigenous lands and oppression of Natives, who were "less than human." This stemmed from two 1454 Papal Bulls of Pope Nicholas V, which justified and even encouraged slavery. The Lakota Country Times reported that, in June 2018, a Jesuit priest and a Lakota tribal elder appealed to Pope Francis, through the Superior General of the Jesuits, to repeal these Bulls. There has been no response from the Vatican so far. So much for the teachings of the Man who preached, "Love thy neighbor as thyself."

- California has the largest Native American population of any State.

- A Cherokee, Joseph James Clark, became an Admiral of the US Navy.

- Brigadier General Stand Wattie, a Comanche, was the very last Confederate General to surrender during the American Civil War.

- Ira Hayes, a Pima, was among the Marines who raised the US flag at Iwo Jima.

- Jim Thorpe, of the Sac & Fox Nation, won gold at the 1912 Stockholm Olympics and was named by the Swedish King, "the world's greatest athlete."

- Cherokee Andy Payne, who used to run 8 miles to school and back every day, won the inaugural 3400 miles Los Angeles to New York City trans-continental foot race, celebrating Route 66, in 84 days.

- Charles Curtis, the 31st Vice President of the United States was from the Kaw Nation of Kansas. He also inherited Osage and Potawatomi blood.

- Will Rogers, the highest-paid Hollywood star and showman of his time, after whom Oklahoma Airport is named, was a Cherokee.

- Today, 56 million acres of land remain "in trust" with the Secretary of the Interior, supposedly for the benefit of the Native Nations. On Thanksgiving Day 2018, during the festival originated by the Wampanoag, the US Congress moved to derecognize one of the Wampanoag tribes, the ones who had helped the original Mayflower Pilgrims survive, and took away their "trust" land.

- There are 576 Federally recognized tribal Nations in the USA, over 334 fractured reservations.

- In its early days, there was an "Indian Village," operated by a group of relocated Natives at Disneyland, Anaheim. However, when they went on strike demanding wage parity with the white performers, Walt's younger brother fired them all and shut down the attraction. Discrimination against Natives springs up in the least expected of places.

A BRIEF READING AND VIEWING LIST

Read

- "Bury my Heart at Wounded Knee" Dee Brown (different from the book)
- "Creek Mary's Blood" Dee Brown
- "Black Elk Speaks" John G. Niehardt
- "The Journey of Crazy Horse: A Lakota History" Joseph M. Marshall III
- "Sacred Fireplace: Oceti Wakan" Pete S. Catches Sr & Peter V. Catches
- "Black Elk Speaks IV" Ed McGaa Eagleman
- "Walking in the Sacred Manner" Mark St. Pierre & Tilda Long Soldier
- "Madonna Swan: A Lakota Woman's Story" Mark St. Pierre
- "Intergenerational Trauma: Understanding Natives' Inherited Pain" Mary Pember
- "Fight the Power: Heroes of Native Resistance" Vincent Schilling
- "The Soul of the Indian" Charles Eastman
- "Blue Highways" William Least Heat-Moon
- "Stone Song" Will Blevins
- "Raven Shadow" Will Blevins
- "The Rock Child" Will Blevins
- "Rendezvous Series 1-6" Will Blevins

- "Charbonneau" Will Blevins
- "Nine Years among the Indians" Herman Lehmann
- "Travels with Charlie in Search of America" John Steinbeck
- "Tales behind the Tombstones" Chris Enss
- "Native Roots: How the Indians Enriched America" Jack Weatherford
- "Sitting Bull and Crazy Horse" Charles Haven Ladd Johnston
- "Red Cloud: The Great Ogllala Sioux War Chief" Grace Hebard, Earl Alonzo Brininstool
- "Empire of the Summer Moon" S.C.Gwynne
- "The Adventures of Buffalo Bill" Colonel William Frederick Cody
- "Custer and Crazy Horse" Stephen Ambrose
- "There There" Tommy Orange
- "The Inconvenient Indian" Thomas King
- "McGillycuddy, Agent" Julia Blanchard
- "Crazy Horse, the Strange Man of the Oglalas" Marie Sandoz
- "Good Friday on the Rez" David Hugh Bunnell
- "Crazy Horse: A Lakota Life" Kingsley Bray
- "Crazy Horse: The Lakota Warrior's Life & Legacy" The Edward Clown Family
- "The North American Indian" Edward Curtis
- "In the Spirit of Crazy Horse" Peter Matthiessen
- "Lakota Noon" Gregory F. Michno
- "The Earth Shall Weep: A History of Native America" James Wilson
- "Geronimo's Story of His Life" Geronimo
- "The Fetterman Massacre: Fort Phil Kearny and the Battle of the 100 Slain" Dee Brown
- "Lakota Woman" Richard Erdoes & Mary Crow Dog

Visit

http://www.cloudhorseartinstitute.org
http://www.ocetiwakan.org
http://www.vizettes.com/kt/native_americans/index.htm
http://www.richcoffeymusic.com/links/na/how-the-west-was-lost.htm

View

- "Seven Sacred Rites of the Lakota" Oceti Wakan
- "The West" Robert Redford
- "The West" Ken Burns (primarily from the Settlers' perspective)
- "Deadwood" TV Series from HBO
- "Geronimo: An American Legend"
- "Bury my Heart at Wounded Knee" (not a replacement for the book)
- "Destiny at Dawn" Washita Battlefield National Historic Site
- "The Great Indian Wars 1540:1890" Mill Creek Entertainment
- "Trail of Tears" Octapixx Worldwide
- "Who Really Killed Crazy Horse" History Channel
- "Reel Injuns"
- "Who Will Bury the Dead" Cloud Horse Art
- "Mallard's Road" Cloud Horse Art

9 789353 912345

Printed at Repro India Ltd.